AQA

KS3

Activate
Know · Apply · Extend
1

Workbook: Higher
Including Diagnostic Pinchpoint activities

Jon Clarke
Philippa Gardom Hulme
Jo Locke

Assessment Editor
Dr Andrew Chandler-Grevatt

OXFORD
UNIVERSITY PRESS

Contents

EP1 Asking scientific questions
EP2 Planning investigations

A Fill in the gaps to complete the sentences.

The plan for an investigation starts with the scientific _____ you are trying to answer. You should

make a _____ about what the answer might be, and use your scientific _____ to

explain your prediction.

In your plan you should identify the _____ variable you will change, the _____

variable you will measure or observe, and a list of variables you will _____. Your plan should

also include a list of the _____ you will use, and your method. You should also include a

_____ _____ to make sure your investigation is as safe as possible.

The measurements or observations you make are called _____. It is important that they are accurate

and _____.

B Write a description for the following types of variable:

a Independent variable _____ _____

b Dependent variable ____ _____

c Control variable _____

C A group of students carry out an investigation to find out if there is a correlation between temperature and the volume of gas produced.

Which type of scientific enquiry question is being investigated?

_____

D For each of the following statements, circle the correct word in **bold**.

The measurements you collect in an investigation are called **variables / data**.

Accurate / precise data is close to the true value of what you are trying to measure.

Accurate / precise data has a very small spread when measurements are repeated.

Measurements are **repeatable / reproducible** if you repeat the experiment several times and get similar results.

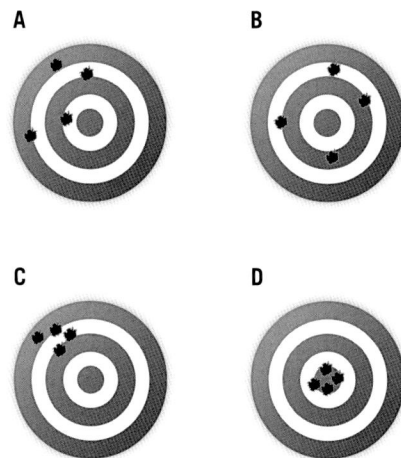

A   B

C   D

E Which of the diagrams on the right could represent data that is not accurate but is precise?

_____

F A student sets light to a piece of magnesium ribbon.

Identify **one** risk and how it can be managed.

_____

_____

EP3 Collecting, recording, and presenting data

A Fill in the gaps to complete the sentences.

Before starting an investigation you should produce a _____ table. You should put the

_____ variable in the first column, and allow space to take repeat _____ and calculate

a _____. Also remember to include _____ in the column headings. Check your data

for _____ – anomalous results, and _____ the measurement.

When plotting a graph, make sure you choose an appropriate _____ and put the independent

variable on the _____-axis. If both the dependent and independent variables are continuous, you

should plot a _____ _____. If your independent variable is categoric you should plot a

_____ _____. You can also display discrete or categoric data in a _____

_____.

B A group of students carried out an investigation to measure how far a toy car travels down slopes of different steepness, every 10° between 0° and 40°. They took repeat readings and calculated a mean.

Add headings, with units, to the table below to produce a results table for the students to collect their results.

C In the investigation in activity **B**, for a slope angle of 30° the students got the following distance readings:

60 cm   **58 cm**   **80 cm**

Circle the reading which is likely to be an **outlier**.

D Calculate the **mean** distance travelled from the data below, collected at a slope of 20°.

Distance ball travelled:	48 cm	50 cm	55 cm

_____ cm

E Sketch an appropriate graph in the space below, which would display all the data the students may have collected.

Hint: Include the data shown in activities **C** and **D**.

EP4 Analysing patterns in data

A Fill in the gaps to complete the sentences.

It is often helpful to plot _____ from an experiment, and draw a line of _____

_____ in order to analyse the results. This might be a straight line or a _____, and goes

as near as possible to as many points as possible. A _____ will state what was found out and any

_____ found between the variables, and use _____ knowledge to explain the pattern

and compare the results with the _____.

B Describe the pattern shown in the graph below.

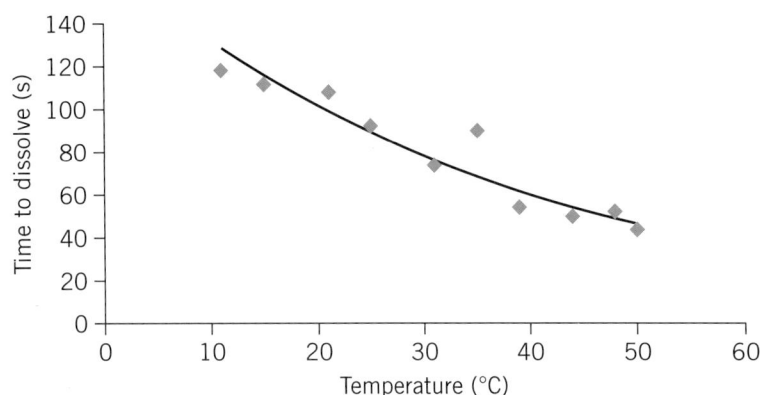

_____

_____

C a A student investigated the extension of a spring. The table shows the data obtained.

Draw a graph of the results below. Plot the data and draw a line of best fit, identifying and labelling any outliers.

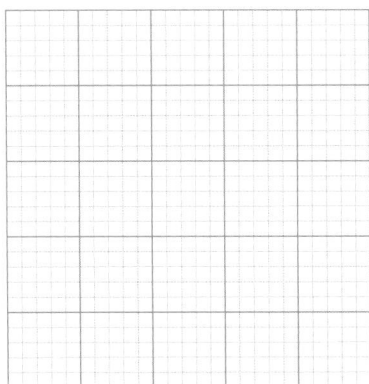

Force (N)	Extension (cm)
1.0	0.5
2.0	1.0
3.0	1.4
4.0	1.8
5.0	2.3
6.0	3.8
7.0	3.3
8.0	3.7

b The student predicted that as force increased it would cause extension to increase. Write a **detailed** conclusion based on the data and your graph.

_____

_____

_____

_____

EP5 Evaluating data and methods

A Fill in the gaps to complete the sentences.

There are two ways to _____ your investigation. You should discuss the _____

of the _____ that you have collected, and suggest and explain _____ to your

_____ so you can collect data of better quality if you repeat the experiment. Your suggested

improvements should increase the _____ that you have in your conclusion. Having few, or no,

_____ in the data increases the confidence in the conclusion. The spread of data tells you how

_____ the data is. Having a small spread in the data will give you _____ confidence

in your conclusion. _____ errors, such as a digital mass balance only reading to the nearest 1 g,

can increase the spread, or cause outliers. _____ errors, such as a newtonmeter reading 1 N even

when there is nothing attached, can reduce the accuracy. You might get better data by including a bigger

_____ of the independent variable, or taking _____ readings.

B Describe the stages in evaluating data from an experiment.

_____

_____

_____

C The table below shows repeated readings of force from two groups, for the same part of the same investigation.

Group One, force (N)	12, 17, 14
Group Two, force (N)	12, 15, 14, 14, 13

   a Compare and contrast the data from the two groups, suggesting **two** reasons why the data may be different.

_____

_____

_____

_____

_____

   b Explain two ways that group 1 could improve their data if they did the investigation again.

_____

_____

_____

_____

Enquiry Processes Pinchpoint ⊗

Pinchpoint question

Answer the question below, then do the follow-up activity **with the same letter** as the answer you picked.

Roland and Amira wanted to find out the effect of light on the number of bubbles produced from a stem of pond weed. They took three measurements at each distance from the lamp.

Their results are shown in the table.

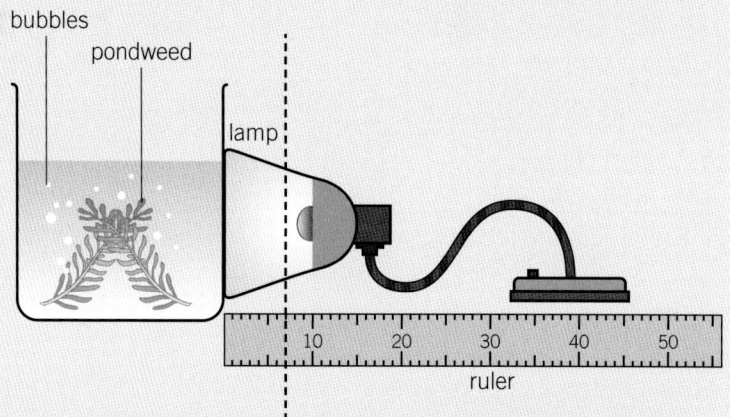

| Distance from lamp (cm) | Number of oxygen bubbles produced in one minute | | | |
	1st measurement	2nd measurement	3rd measurement	Mean
0	10	22	25	19
10	11	15	18	15
20	6	6	7	6
30	5	2	1	3
40	1	2	1	1

They conclude that the greater the distance from the lamp, the fewer bubbles are produced.

Which evaluation is best for these data?

We could increase our confidence in our conclusion by:

A   changing one of the variables.

B   repeating each measurement 5 times to reduce uncertainty in the results.

C   increasing the number of readings by measuring at 5 cm intervals.

D   trying to increase the spread of the results to improve precision.

Follow-up activities

A   Draw a line to match each feature of investigation to its definition.

Type of feature	Definition
accurate	This describes a set of repeat measurements that are close together.
precise	When you take the measurements of an investigation again and get similar results.
repeatable	When other people carry out the same investigation and get similar measurements.
reproducible	Close to the true value of what you are measuring.

Hint: Make sure you know the difference between these key words. See EP2 Planning investigations and the Student Book Glossary for help.

B The table shows improvements that can made to a practical investigation.
Tick which improvements improve accuracy and which improve precision.

	Improvement	Accuracy	Precision
1	Change the measuring equipment to one that takes finer readings		
2	Aim to reduce the spread of results		
3	The same person takes the measurements		
4	Check the equipment is set to zero, e.g. a balance or forcemeter		
5	Repeat the measurements more often and remove the outliers		

Hint: Make sure you know the difference between accuracy and precision. See EP2 Planning investigations and EP5 Evaluating data and methods for help.

C **a** Suggest two reasons why counting gas bubbles can be inaccurate.

1 _____

2 _____

b Suggest a way to improve the accuracy of the experiment.

_____

_____

_____

Hint: See EP2 Planning investigations and EP5 Evaluating data and methods for help.

D Tick the ways in which you could change the investigation to get better data.

1 Get someone else to do the experiment ☐

2 Take readings more often, e.g. every 5 cm instead of every 10 cm ☐

3 Change one of the variables, e.g. the type of pond weed ☐

4 Take more readings, e.g. 5 readings instead of 3 ☐

5 Use more accurate apparatus, e.g. gas syringes to measure volume of gas ☐

6 Identify outliers ☐

Hint: Focus on improving the data you collect. See EP5 Evaluating data and methods for help.

⊗ Pinchpoint review

Now look back at the question – do you think you chose the right letter?
Turn to the Answers page to find out.

1.1.1 Introduction to forces

A Fill in the gaps to complete the sentences.

A force can be a _____ or a _____. Forces explain why objects _____ in the way that they do. They can change the _____ that objects are moving in, and change their _____. They might be a non-contact force, such as _____, or a contact force, such as _____ or _____. Forces always come in pairs, called _____ pairs. Forces can be _____ with a newtonmeter. All forces are measured in _____.

B Draw a line to match each sentence's start to a correct middle and ending.

| A force of friction | of the Earth on the water | helps a skydiver land safely. |

| A force of air resistance | of the road on the tyre | makes spilt water spread into a puddle. |

| A force of gravity | of the air on their parachute | makes a bus change speed. |

C Explain the difference between a contact force, such as air resistance, and a non-contact force, such as gravity.

_____

_____

_____

D A fridge magnet is a decorative item that sticks to the side of a fridge, often to hold paper or photographs in place.

a Suggest which forces you think are acting on the magnet. For each of them, draw and label a force arrow on this diagram.

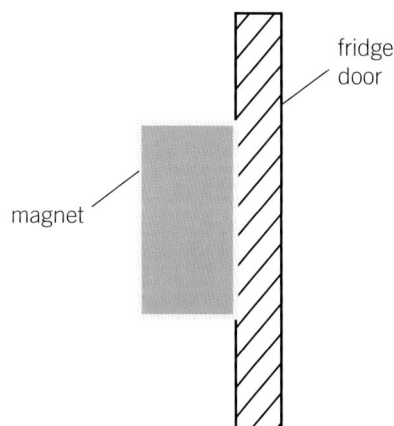

fridge door

magnet

b Choose **one** of the forces on the magnet, and suggest which force completes its interaction pair.

Force: _____

Force that completes the pair: _____

1.1.2 Balanced and unbalanced

A Fill in the gaps to complete the sentences.

A force pushing an object along, such as the effect of a car engine, is called a _____ force.

A force that tends to slow an object down, such as air resistance, is called a _____ force.

The _____ of all the forces on an object is called the _____ force. If the resultant

force is _____, the forces are balanced and the object is in equilibrium.

B Describe two situations that are in equilibrium, identifying the forces involved and what condition is true about them.

1 _____

_____

2 _____

_____

C **a** Add force arrows to this diagram to show balanced forces.

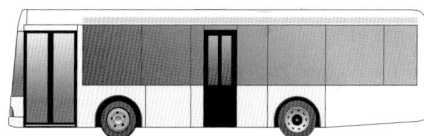

b Add force arrows to this diagram to show unbalanced forces.

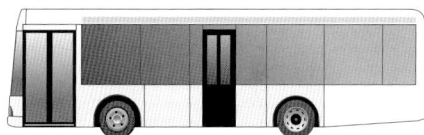

c Explain the difference between balanced and unbalanced forces using your examples.

_____

_____

_____

D The diagram shows the only force acting on the Moon. Use the concept of resultant force to suggest why the Moon orbits the Earth in circles.

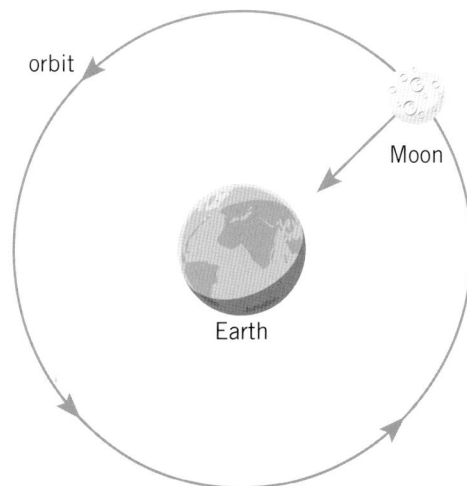

_____

_____

_____

_____

_____

1.1.3 Speed

A Fill in the gaps to complete the sentences.

The rate at which something moves is called _____. It is defined and calculated as the

_____ travelled (m) divided by the time taken (s). It has the unit _____

_____ _____, symbol m/s. If something moves a _____ of

one metre in one second, then it has a _____ of one m/s. We can distinguish between the

_____ that something has just at one moment – its _____ _____ –

and its _____ _____ over a whole journey. When two objects are moving, we can

talk about their _____ _____. For instance, two people walking at the same speed

of 1.5 m/s would have a _____ _____ of zero if they are walking in the same

direction, but a _____ _____ of 3 m/s if they are walking in opposite directions.

B Average speed can be calculated if you know the distance travelled and the time taken. Recall the formula for speed to answer these questions.

   a A motorbike drives a distance of 500 m in a time of 30 s.

      Calculate its average speed.

                                                                                                      _____

   b The formula for speed can be used with different units.

      A train travels 160 km in 2.0 h. Calculate the average speed.

                                                                                                   _____

   c Rearrange the formula for speed to calculate the distance travelled. The sound of thunder travels at 330 m/s. Calculate how far it will travel in 12 s.

                                                                                                   _____

C One type of traffic speed camera works by taking a pair of photographs 0.50 s apart while the traffic drives over equally spaced, parallel white lines on the road.

The speed limit on the motorway is 31 metres per second (m/s). One pair of photographs shows that a car travelled 20 m in the time between the photographs.

   a Calculate the speed of the car.

                                                                                                   _____

   b Was the car exceeding the speed limit?

      _____

D An airliner is cruising at 900 km/h. Describe and explain how the motion of the airliner looks to:

   a someone stationary, standing on the ground.

      _____

      _____

   b someone on another airliner flying nearby in the same direction at the same speed.

      _____

      _____

1.1.4 Distance–time graphs

A Fill in the gaps to complete the sentences.

One way to describe a journey is to plot a _____–_____ graph. If an object is not

moving, the graph stays _____. The slope of the graph shows its _____. If the object's

speed is changing, we say it is _____.

B Lola carries out an experiment on a wind-up moving toy, measuring the distance it travels three times.

a Her results are shown in the table below.

Time (s)	Distance 1st reading (m)	Distance 2nd reading (m)	Distance 3rd reading (m)	Average distance (m)
0	0.00	0.00	0.00	
5	0.04	0.02	0.05	
10	0.11	0.12	0.12	
15	0.26	0.31	0.26	
20	0.43	0.48	0.40	
25	0.60	0.63	0.58	
30	0.75	0.80	0.74	
35	0.78	0.83	0.80	
40	0.78	0.83	0.81	

i Complete the table by calculating the average distance for each time.

ii Plot the data on the axes given and draw a smooth line of best fit.

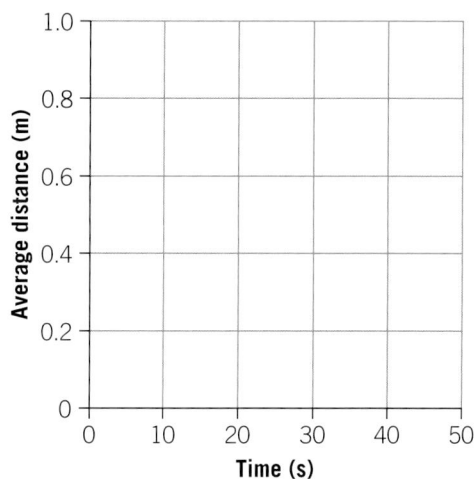

b Describe what is happening to the toy between:

i 0 s and 10 s

_____

_____

ii 10 s and 30 s

_____

_____

iii 30 s and 40 s.

_____

_____

c Calculate the maximum speed of the toy from the graph.

1.2.1 Gravity

A Fill in the gaps to complete the sentences.

_____ are regions where an object experiences a _____ force, such as gravitational,

magnetic, or electrostatic forces. For instance, around a _____ there is an electrostatic field. If another

_____ comes into that field, it experiences a force, and the force gets _____ the closer

it comes.

Every object exerts a _____ force on every other object. It increases with mass and

_____ with distance. Weight is the force of _____ on an object. You can calculate

weight using the equation: weight (N) = _____ (kg) x gravitational field strength, g (N/kg)

B Circle the correct **bold** phrases in the sentences below.

A field is a region where something experiences **an acceleration / friction / a force**. Around the Earth there

is a gravitational field where **magnets / masses / electrical charges** experience a force due to gravity. As an

object gets further from the Earth, the field **stays the same / gets stronger / gets weaker**, so that the force

on the object becomes smaller.

C The table shows the strength of the gravitational field in different places. A value of 1 N/kg means that a mass of
1 kg experiences a gravitational force (a weight) of 1 N. An astronaut and her equipment have a mass of 160 kg.
Complete the table by calculating the weight of the astronaut in each place.

Place	Gravitational field strength (N/kg)	Weight of astronaut and her equipment (N)
the Earth's surface	9.8	
in orbit around the Earth	8.7	
the Moon's surface	1.6	
far from any star or planet	0.0	

D a Lightning is caused by charges in a thundercloud creating an electrostatic field.

Suggest why it is more dangerous to stand on a high building than on the ground during a thunderstorm.

_____

_____

b Give one similarity and one difference between the electrostatic field in a thunderstorm and the gravitational
field that keeps a satellite orbiting the Earth.

Similarity _____

Difference _____

E The Voyager 1 space probe was launched in 1977. It has been travelling away from the Earth and Sun ever since,
and is now the most distant man-made object.

Describe and explain any changes to the gravitational force on the probe due to the Earth.

_____

_____

_____

Pinchpoint question

Answer the question below, then do the follow-up activity **with the same letter** as the answer you picked.

A bicycle is turning a corner to the left. It is changing direction but not speed.

Circle which diagram and statement best describes the situation.

A

driving force

turning force ← → resistive forces

resistive forces

The forces are balanced.

B

driving force

turning force ←

resistive forces

The forces are unbalanced.

C

driving force

turning force ← → resistive forces

resistive forces

The forces are unbalanced.

D

driving force

turning force ←

resistive forces

The forces are balanced.

Follow-up activities

A Forces must be unbalanced to change an object's motion.

  a Marianne holds a ball in her hand. There are two forces acting on the ball.

    i Draw and label the force arrows on this diagram.

    ii Are the forces balanced? _____

    iii Is the motion of the ball changing? _____

  b She now takes her hand away, dropping the ball. Think about which forces – if any – are now acting on the ball.

    i Draw and label force arrows – if any – on this diagram.

    ii Are the forces balanced? _____

    iii Is the motion of the ball changing? _____

  Hint: Can balanced forces change motion? For help see 1.1.2 Balanced and unbalanced.

B To move in a circle, an object must have an unbalanced force acting on it, pointing in a particular direction.

    a A cyclist rides around a roundabout. Draw on the diagram the direction of the turning force.

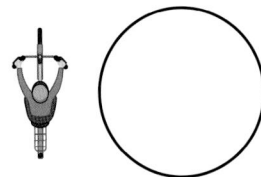

    b The cyclist continues around the roundabout. Draw on the diagram the direction of the turning force.

    Hint: Is turning a corner a change in motion? For help see 1.1.2 Balanced and unbalanced.

C Every force has an interaction pair, but for unbalanced forces, the paired force is on a **different** object.

In the example of the turning cyclist in the Pinchpoint question, the turning force is the road pushing the cyclist to the left.

    a Give the other force in that interaction pair. _____

    b The diagram shows someone pushing a box, showing the arrow for that force. Draw a force arrow to show the interaction pair for the person pushing the box.

    c Which object is your force arrow acting on? _____

    Hint: What is the definition of balanced forces? For help see 1.1.2 Balanced and unbalanced.

D Motion cannot change for an object with balanced forces on it. Forces must be unbalanced to change motion.

For each diagram below:

-    write whether the forces are **balanced** or **unbalanced**,
-    write whether motion will **change** or **not** change
-    if motion will change, write whether the object will turn **left** or **right**, **speed up**, or **slow down**.

    a _____

    b _____

    Hint: What is the definition of balanced forces? For help see 1.1.2 Balanced and unbalanced.

Pinchpoint review

Now look back at the question – do you think you chose the right letter?
Turn to the Answers page to find out.

2.1.1 Potential difference

A Fill in the gaps to complete the sentences.

A component that can push charge around a circuit is a _____ or _____.

This 'push' is called the _____ _____. We use a _____ to measure

potential difference. It must be connected in _____ so that it is across the component we are

interested in. Potential difference is measured in _____, with symbol_____, so

potential difference is often known as _____. Cells and batteries are given a _____,

which is the potential difference across the cell / battery. A _____ potential difference means

that more _____is transferred to the components in a circuit than if the potential difference is

_____.

B **a** Draw a circuit diagram to show how you would measure potential difference across a bulb.

b Fill in the gaps to complete the sentences about potential difference.

Potential difference (p.d.) means the 'push' provided by the _____ (that is, the energy that it can

provide). Another term commonly used for p.d. is _____. The amount of potential difference that

a _____ provides is measured in _____.

C Draw a line to match each variable with its properties and behaviour in a series circuit.

Current		Total for all components same as rating for cell		Relates to charge flowing

Potential difference		Same everywhere		Relates to energy transferred to a component

D The diagram shows a simple circuit.

The bulb is kept the same in this circuit. Suggest what happens to the bulb if the cell is replaced by one with a:

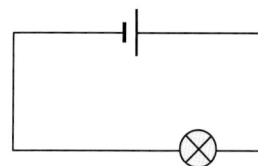

a lower rating _____

b higher rating _____

E Explain why a voltmeter must be connected in parallel.

_____

_____

_____

_____

2.1.2 Resistance

A Fill in the gaps to complete the sentences.

_____ is a measure of how much 'push' is required to get current through a component. Strictly, it

is defined and calculated as the _____ _____ across a component divided by the

_____ through that component. It has the unit _____ , symbol Ω. If 1 V applied across

a component causes 1 A to flow, we say that the component has a _____ of 1 Ω. Electrical insulators

have very _____ resistance and electrical conductors have very _____ resistance.

B Resistance can be calculated using the following formula:

$$\text{resistance } (\Omega) = \frac{\text{potential difference (V)}}{\text{current (A)}}$$

Calculate the resistance of the bulb in the circuit shown to the right. Give the unit.

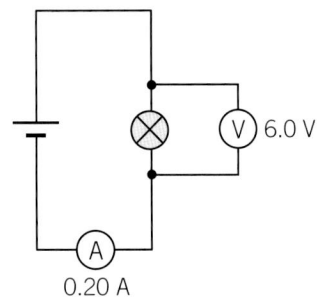

_____

6.0 V

0.20 A

C **a** Rearrange the formula for resistance to give the formula for calculating current.

_____

b Calculate the current flowing through this cell.

$R = 30\ \Omega$ 9.0 V

_____

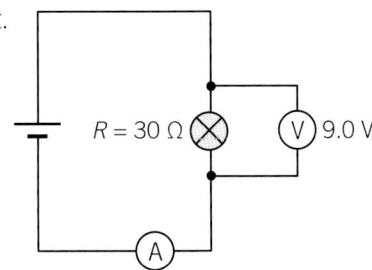

D **a** Rearrange the formula for resistance to calculate potential difference.

_____

b Calculate the potential difference across this bulb.

$R = 20\ \Omega$

_____

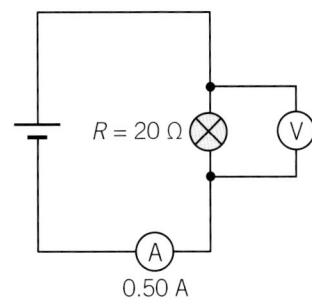

E One problem with the copper metal used to make electrical wires is that it has some
resistance.

Explain the cause of this resistance.

0.50 A

_____

_____

F Draw a line to link each factor with its effect on the resistance of a wire and the explanation.

| Increasing length of wire | decreases resistance | because there are more paths along which the electrons can travel through the vibrating particles |
| Increasing diameter of wire | increases resistance | because each electron collides with more vibrating particles as it passes along the wire |

G Explain how and why the resistance of the wiring in a hairdryer differs from the resistance of its outer plastic coating.

_____

_____

2.1.3 Series and parallel circuits

A Fill in the gaps to complete the sentences.

There are two types of electrical circuits. _____ circuits have all their components, including the

cell, in one loop. If you add up the _____ _____ across each component, the sum

is equal to the _____ _____ across the cell. _____ circuits have their

components in more than one loop. The _____ _____ across each loop is the same

as that across the cell.

B The diagrams below show some simple series and parallel circuits, including some readings on voltmeters.
Write in the missing readings.

a

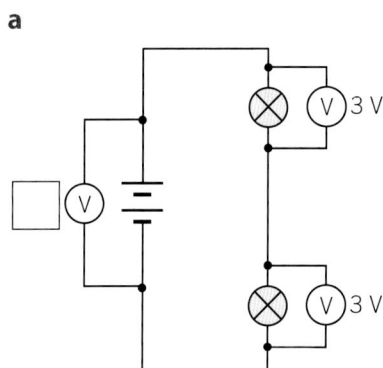

b

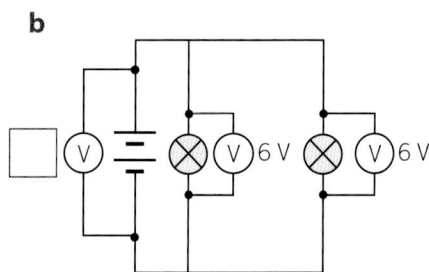

C A series circuit consists of a battery and two 10 Ω resistors. One of the resistors is replaced with a 20 Ω resistor.

Predict the effect on the total resistance of the circuit.

_____

D The law of conservation of energy says that energy cannot be created or destroyed. In a circuit, potential difference
relates to the amount of energy transferred from the cell to the components in the circuit.

Suggest how this law applies to potential difference in each type of circuit.

Series _____

_____

Parallel _____

_____

Hint: For more on conservation of energy, see 3.2.1 Energy adds up.

2.2.1 Current

A Fill in the gaps to complete the sentences.

Negatively charged _____ move when current flows in a metal. Current is the amount of charge

flowing per _____. We use an _____ to measure current in an electrical circuit.

It must be connected in _____ so that all of the current that flows through the component of

interest also flows through the _____. The unit of current is the ampere, often abbreviated to

_____, with the symbol _____. A component that can make an object move is a

_____ . A device that can break and complete a circuit is a _____. A circuit must be

_____ for the charge to flow around it.

B A scientist decides to investigate the amount of electrical current needed to power different types of light bulb. She sets up a circuit for each lightbulb as shown.

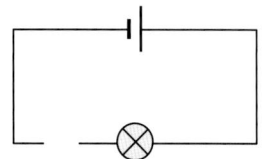

   a Complete the circuit to show how she can measure the current that the bulb needs.

   b Tick the correct way in which the component in part **a** needs to be added to the circuit:

    series   ☐   parallel   ☐

   c Define the term 'current'.

   _____

C **a** The diagram shows a simple circuit.

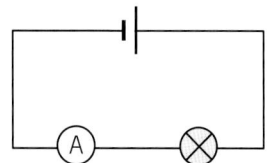

     The cell in this circuit is kept the same while more bulbs are added in series.

     What will happen to the current in this circuit?

     _____

   b Fill in the missing ammeter reading for this circuit.

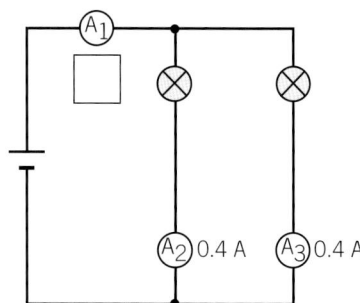

D **a** One model of electricity uses a loop of rope as shown.

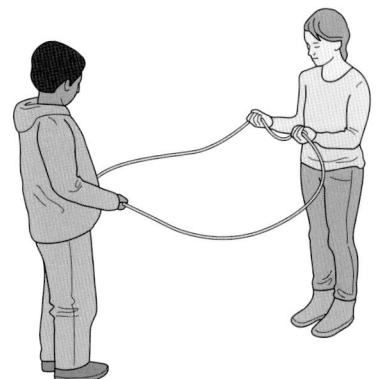

     One person acts as a cell, pulling the rope around, through the hands of the person acting as a bulb.

     i What electrical concept does a piece of the rope represent?

       _____

     ii What represents current in the model?

       _____

   b The person acting as a bulb represents greater resistance by gripping the rope harder so that the rope moves more slowly. Describe what has changed in terms of the charges in the circuit.

     _____

2.2.2 Charging up

A Fill in the gaps to complete the sentences.

Atoms contain equal numbers of _____ (+) and _____ (−), so overall, atoms

have a _____ charge. When two objects are rubbed together, _____ moves

_____ from one object to the other, making one object _____ charged and the other

object positively charged. We say that both objects are now charged up. Charged objects are surrounded by an

_____ _____ , which causes an _____ force. If two charged objects

have the same type of charge, they _____ each other. If two charged objects have the opposite type

of charge (one + and one −), they _____ each other. Thunderstorms generate very strong electric

fields, which cause _____ .

B **a** Complete the sentences below to explain how objects can become charged.

Atoms are made of positive and negative particles. _____ separates charge. When the objects

are rubbed together, this moves _____ from one material to the other. The material that lost

_____ now has _____ charge overall. The other material has _____

charge.

b A series of objects have been charged with friction.
Complete the table to show which pairs of objects will attract, repel, or have no effect on each other.

Pair	1st object charge	2nd object charge	Attract, repel, or no effect?
A	positive	positive	
B	positive	negative	
C	negative	positive	
D	negative	negative	

C Static electricity can be used to improve spray painting of a car in a factory, as shown in this diagram.

a Circle what happens as the neutral paint droplets pass the positive tip of the spray gun.

paint droplets gain electrons   nothing

paint droplets lose electrons

nozzle of spray gun is positively charged

paint particles become positively charged

the car has a negative charge

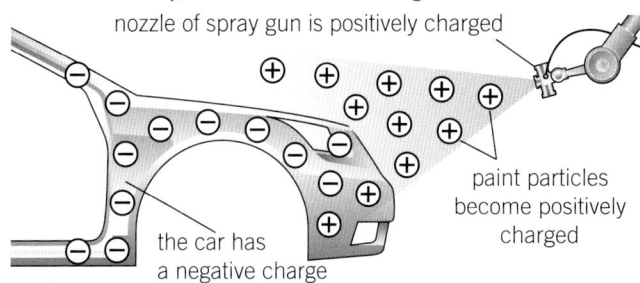

b **i** Circle a prediction for how the charged paint particles will interact with the car.

paint droplets attracted to car   **paint droplets neither attracted nor repelled**

paint droplets repelled by car

ii Suggest why this technique is better than spray painting without using electricity.

_____

D Sometimes people experience an electric shock when climbing out of a car after a journey, especially after they slide their clothes across the car seat. Suggest why this occurs.

_____

_____

Pinchpoint question

Answer the question below, then do the follow-up activity **with the same letter** as the answer you picked.

The circuits in the diagrams below include identical bulbs and cells.

Choose the statement that correctly describes and explains the behaviour of electricity in the circuits.

A In both circuits, the current at **X** must be less than the current at **W** because it is used up going through the bulbs.

B Each bulb in the series circuit is brighter than each bulb in the parallel circuit, because all of the current from the cell goes through them.

C The voltmeter reading V_1 must be greater than the voltmeter reading V_2 because each charge has to do more work (transfer more energy) to get through more bulbs.

D In the parallel circuit on the right, the current at **Y** and at **Z** must add up to the current reading at **W**, because electrical charge cannot be created or destroyed.

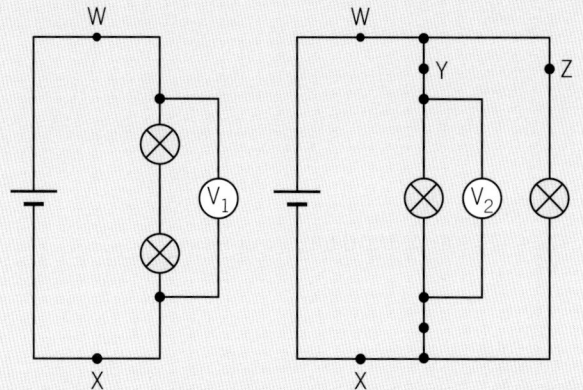

Follow-up activities

A In a series circuit, the current must be the same everywhere.

Complete the statements below to explain why.

Like energy, charge cannot be _____ or _____, so charge cannot be used up.

If some charge goes into a bulb, then the _____ amount of charge must come out.

Current is the amount of charge _____ per _____.

If some current goes into a bulb, then the _____ amount of current must come out.

As charge cannot be 'used up', neither can _____.

Hint: What is current? See 2.2.1 Current for help.

B For each question about circuits below, circle your answer.

a In a series circuit, what is the effect on **resistance** of adding more bulbs?

increase / no change / decrease

b In a series circuit, the potential difference across the battery is kept the same. What is the effect on **current** of adding more bulbs?

increase / no change / decrease

c In the diagram below, how does the resistance of the one-bulb branch compare to the two-bulb branch?

higher / same / lower

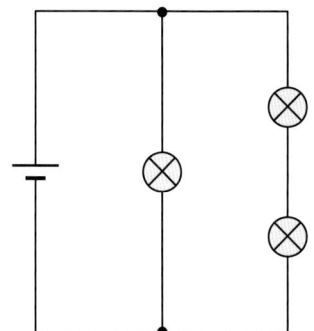

d In the circuit below, how does the voltage reading of V_1 compare to V_2?

higher / same / lower

Hint: How does current depend on resistance? See 2.1.2 Resistance for help.

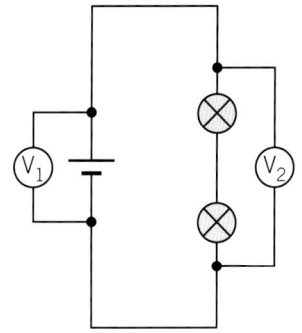

C a Define potential difference.

_____

b Each statement below contains a mistake. Rewrite each statement to correct it.

i Potential difference tells you nothing about energy.

_____

ii The potential difference across all branches of a parallel circuit must be different.

_____

iii Any one electron must do less work on the components than the work the battery did on it.

_____

iv The p.d. across all branches in a circuit sometimes adds up to the p.d. across the cell.

_____

Hint: What is potential difference? See 2.1.1 Potential difference for help.

D In this circuit, the bulbs are all identical, the cell is rated at 3.0 V, and there is 1.2 A of current through the cell.

a What is the potential difference across each of the bulbs? Explain your answer.

_____

_____

b What is the current through each of the bulbs? Explain your answer.

_____

_____

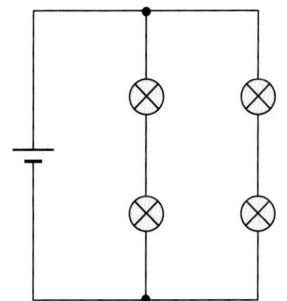

Hint: How do current and potential difference behave in series and parallel circuits? See 2.1.3 Series and parallel circuits for help.

Pinchpoint review

Now look back at the question – do you think you chose the right letter?
Turn to the Answers page to find out.

3.1.1 Food and fuels

A Fill in the gaps to complete the sentences.

Different foods are stores of different amounts of _____. The unit for this is the _____,

and 1000 of them make up one _____. A healthy diet will take in just as much energy as is needed

for the person's _____. The body will convert extra food into _____ to store unused

energy.

B **a** Draw a line to match each activity with its energy requirement.

   b Explain the different energy requirements for sleeping and running.

_____

_____

Sleeping	300 kJ per hour
Running	600 kJ per hour
Working	3600 kJ per hour

C **a** Katie requires 300 kJ of energy to run 1 kilometre.
Calculate the energy she requires for a 20 km training run.

_____

   b Suggest a meal that meets Katie's energy requirements, using the data in the table.

_____

_____

_____

Food	Energy (kJ) per 100 g
apple	200
banana	340
chicken breast	600
whole wheat pasta	700
chocolate	1500
dried fruit and nut mix	1900

   c Katie is preparing to run a 160 km 'ultramarathon'. She will need to consume half of the required energy while running and so wants the food to take up a small volume.

     i Calculate how much energy she needs to consume while running.

_____ kJ

     ii Suggest the mass of a low-volume food she could eat while running.

_____ g of _____

D A dietician wants to calculate how much energy is needed by a child in one day.

Aiden walks for one hour (800 kJ/h), works for six hours (600 kJ/h), relaxes for five hours (360 kJ/h) and sleeps for twelve hours (300 kJ/h).

Complete the table and calculate the total energy needed for one day.

Activity	Duration (hours)	Energy required for an hour of activity (kJ/h)	Total energy used (kJ)
walking	1		
working	6		
relaxing	5		
sleeping	12		

Total energy used in 24 hours: _____

3.1.2 Energy resources

A Fill in the gaps to complete the sentences.

Anything that can be used as a fuel or to generate electricity is an _____ _____.

Coal, oil, and gas are examples of _____ _____. These cannot be readily replaced,

so they are _____. Some energy resources such as wind and solar are continually being produced

and are _____. When fossil fuels are burnt, they produce _____ _____

which contributes to climate change and _____ _____ which contributes to acid rain.

When renewable sources such as wind and solar are in use, they do not produce these polluting gases.

B **a** Name an energy resource that can be used in a thermal power station, other than coal.

_____

b Write the order of these statements which gives the best description of how coal is used in a thermal power station to generate electricity for your home.

Correct order ☐ ☐ ☐ ☐ ☐ ☐

   1 steam, which drives a…

   2 Coal is burnt, which heats…

   3 electrical current to power your home

   4 turbine, which turns a…

   5 water, to produce…

   6 generator, which pushes…

C List the advantages of using renewable and non-renewable resources, giving at least one advantage for each.

_____

_____

_____

_____

D You are the adviser to the Prime Minister. Your country has increased its use of electricity for each of the previous ten years. It is now at risk of exceeding the capacity of its existing power stations.

Suggest what action the Prime Minister could take, and justify how your suggestion will not add to global warming.

_____

_____

_____

23

3.1.3 Energy and power

A Fill in the gaps to complete the sentences.

Power (in W) is defined and calculated as the _____ transferred (J) divided by the

_____ taken for that transfer (s). If one joule of _____ is transferred in one second,

then the _____ produced is one watt (W). In electrical circuits, power can be calculated as the

_____ times the _____ _____. Electrical devices are often labelled with

a _____ _____. This shows the amount of power they can produce. The unit for this is

the _____ with the symbol W, and 1000 of them make up one _____, symbol kW.

If you use a device that produces one kilowatt of power for one hour, you will have transferred one

_____ _____ of energy, symbol kW h.

B Recall the correct equation for each of the questions below.

    a   A gas stove runs for 30 s and burns fuel of energy 45 000 J.
          Calculate the power produced by the gas stove.

                                          _____

    b   **i**   A hairdryer requires a current of 10 A and operates at 230 V.
              Calculate the power produced by the hairdryer.

                                            _____

        ii   Calculate how much energy is transferred by the hairdryer in 30 s.

                                            _____

    c   An electrical radiator to heat a room is rated at 2 kW.
          Calculate the energy transferred when the radiator heats a room for four hours.

                                            _____

C Harper lights her front room with a 75 W light bulb. It is on for 4 hours per day and Harper pays 15 p per kW h
for electricity.

    a   Calculate the cost in pence of using the bulb for one year. There are 365 days in a year.

                                            _____

    b   An LED bulb of equivalent brightness has a power of 11 W.
          Calculate the cost in pence of using an LED bulb for one year.

                                            _____

    c   Calculate the reduction in Harper's energy bill, in pounds, if she uses an LED bulb instead.

3.2.1 Energy adds up

A Fill in the gaps to complete the sentences.

Energy cannot be created or destroyed – this is the law of _____ of _____.

Energy transfers between _____ _____, with some stores emptying as others

_____, so that the _____ amount of energy remains the same. Chemicals, such

as fuels or food and the oxygen needed to combust or respire, have a _____ energy store

associated with them. Hot objects are associated with a _____ energy store; moving ones

with a _____ energy store; objects above the surface of the Earth with a _____

_____ energy store; stretched or compressed ones with an _____ energy store.

B For each situation below, name the energy stores involved.

a Coal is burnt to heat some water.

_____

b Georgia starts her petrol car. It begins to move and then speeds up.

_____

c Charlie freewheels down a hill on his scooter.

_____

C a A ski lift is powered by a petrol-driven engine, and lifts a skier from the foot of a mountain to its top.

    i Suggest which energy stores are involved and whether each fills or empties.

_____

_____

    ii Name which of these stores accounts for energy dissipation.

_____

b A power station burns coal. The electricity it produces is used to power a lift, moving two people from the ground floor to the fifth floor of a building.

    i Describe a form of energy transfer involved in this process.

_____

    ii Explain how the changes in the energy stores obey conservation of energy.

_____

_____

D David is conducting an experiment to measure the effect of energy dissipation when heating a saucepan of water using different heating methods. David times how long it takes for the temperature of the water to increase by 20 °C. For each source of error, circle whether it is systematic or random, and suggest how to minimise it.

Source of error	Systematic or random?	How to minimise error
Left lid off saucepan	systematic / random	
Thermometer reading	systematic / random	
Timing	systematic / random	

3.2.2 Energy dissipation

A Fill in the gaps to complete the sentences.

In many processes, energy is not only transferred to the store you want it in, but also 'lost' to a store which is not

useful. We say that that energy has _____. For instance, when heating the water in a kettle, energy

might not only be transferred to the _____ energy store associated with the water, but also heat the

room, filling the room's _____ energy store, which is not useful.

B a Draw a line to match each situation with a way of reducing the amount of energy dissipated.

i Keeping the inside of a fridge cold		**1** streamlining
ii Moving one part of an engine past another		**2** insulating
iii Driving a vehicle through the air		**3** lubricating

b Explain how energy is dissipated when a toaster heats a slice of bread. Use each of these keywords at least once:

| **heats** | **thermal energy store** | **surroundings** |

_____

_____

C a A bulb takes an input of 9.0 W of electrical power and 8.2 W of its power output is wasted as heat.

i Calculate how much of its power output is useful lighting.

_____

ii Calculate the efficiency of the light bulb.

_____

b When a person does exercise, their muscles dissipate about 3 J of energy into the body's thermal energy store for each 1 J of useful work they do.

i Calculate how much thermal energy is dissipated when a person does 2000 J of work climbing one flight of stairs.

_____

ii Calculate the efficiency of the person's muscles.

_____

D One suggestion to reduce climate change is to introduce more electric transport. A particular fossil fuel, liquified natural gas (LNG), can fuel a car engine with an efficiency of 20%. Burning the same natural gas in a power plant produces electricity, which can be used by an electric car with an efficiency of 50%.

Explain which method is better at reducing dissipation.

_____

_____

Pinchpoint question

Answer the question below, then do the follow-up activity **with the same letter** as the answer you picked.

Parker lives in a remote area and it is winter. He uses an electrical generator that burns diesel fuel to power the electrical devices in his home, including his heaters. The thermostat keeps his home at a constant temperature.

Which statement about the energy transfers involved in one hour of running the generator is correct? The house remains at the temperature set by the thermostat during this time.

A The chemical energy store of the fuel is used up to fill the thermal energy store of the house. As the house cools, the thermal energy store of the house is used up. The thermal store outside the home does not change.

B The chemical energy store of the fuel empties as the current from the generator does work on the heaters. The thermal store of the surroundings fills due to heating from the warm home, filling by as much as the chemical store empties.

C Parker has plugged in his mobile phone to charge it. This fills the electrical energy store of the phone battery.

D The chemical energy store of the fuel empties. The heaters fill the thermal store of the house. The increase in the thermal store of the house is equal to the loss from the chemical store.

Follow-up activities

A Complete the sentences using the keywords below. You may use each word more than once.

constant	fill	warmer	rate	empties	heated	fills

a The diagram shows a hot saucepan that has been put in cooler water.

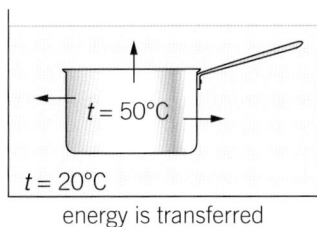

energy is transferred

The saucepan is _____ than the water. The water will be _____ by the saucepan.

The thermal energy store of the saucepan _____ and the thermal energy store of the water

_____. Whenever a thermal energy store empties, another store must _____.

b A house with a thermostat stays at a constant temperature. This means the thermal energy store of the house

stays at a _____ level. Once the house has reached the temperature set by the thermostat,

as the chemical energy store of the fuel _____, energy is transferred into and out of the

house's thermal energy store at the same _____. The thermal energy store of the surroundings

_____ because the house is _____ than its surroundings.

Hint: What is a thermal energy store? See 3.2.1 Energy adds up for help.

B Parker sets the house's thermostats to a higher temperature. Describe and explain the effect this has on the thermal store of the surroundings.

_____

_____

_____

_____

Hint: Which stores change and why? See 3.2.1 Energy adds up for help.

C Complete the sentences about the house using the words below. You may use each word more than once.

store	dissipation	fuel	thermal
work	surroundings	water	chemical

The electrical circuits in the house are just a way for the generator to do _____ on various devices, such as the heater. Electricity is not a _____ of energy in this situation.

When Parker boils a kettle of water, the _____ energy store of the _____ is emptying and the _____ energy store of the _____ is filling. When he recharges his phone battery, the _____ energy store of the _____ is emptying and the _____ energy store of the battery is filling. In both cases, there is also _____, as the thermal energy store of the _____ fills.

Hint: Which energy stores are involved with a generator? See 3.1.2 Energy resources for help.

D Several electrical heaters are used to heat Parker's house. They are controlled by thermostats so that after one hour the house is still at the same temperature.

Circle whether each statement is true or false.

a Heating involves a hotter object (the house) heating a cooler object (the surroundings). **true / false**

b The temperature of the house is different after one hour. **true / false**

c The amount of energy in an object's thermal energy store relates to its temperature. **true / false**

d If the temperature of an object changes, the amount of energy in its thermal energy store does not change. **true / false**

e The house is hotter than its surroundings so the thermal energy store of the surroundings will increase. **true / false**

f After an hour, the thermal energy store of the house will be filling and emptying at a constant rate. **true / false**

Hint: Which stores are involved in heating? See 3.2.1 Energy adds up for help.

⊗ Pinchpoint review

Now look back at the question – do you think you chose the right letter?
Turn to the Answers page to find out.

4.1.1 Sound waves and speed

A Fill in the gaps to complete the sentences.

An object must _____ to cause a sound wave. As it moves backwards and forwards, it causes _____ in the medium to do the same. Sound needs a medium, whether solid, liquid, or gas, to travel through. It cannot travel through a _____. Sound travels fastest in a _____ – this is because the particles in a solid are closer together than in a liquid or a gas, so the vibration is passed along more _____. _____ travels almost a million times faster than sound and does not need a _____ to travel through.

B Explain why the speed of sound in solids is different from the speed of sound in gases, using each of the following keywords at least once.

vibration	medium	solid	gas	sound wave	faster	particles

_____

_____

_____

_____

C Concorde was a **supersonic** passenger plane that operated until 2003. Several aeroplane manufacturers are currently trying to develop a new one. Explain what supersonic travel means.

_____

D Some fireworks use an explosion to produce a bright flash and a loud bang.

Compare and explain the time taken for an observer to hear and see the explosion of a firework.

_____

_____

E We can see the Sun (on a cloudless day). Explain why we will never hear the Sun on Earth.

_____

_____

_____

4.1.2 Loudness and amplitude

A Fill in the gaps to complete the sentences.

The top of a wave is called a _____ or _____, and the bottom of a wave is called a

_____. The distance from the _____ to the _____ of a wave is called

the amplitude. _____ is the distance from one point on a wave to the same point on the next wave.

Frequency is the number of _____ that go past a particular point per _____.

In a longitudinal wave, the _____ of the particles is _____ to the direction of the wave.

You can display a sound wave on an _____ screen. When a wave hits a soft material, it is usually

_____, decreasing the amplitude. When a wave hits a hard material, it is usually _____.

The reflection of a sound is called an _____.

B This diagram shows a sound wave.

Add two arrows to this diagram, with labels, to show
the direction of the wave's motion and the direction of
oscillation of one of the air particles.

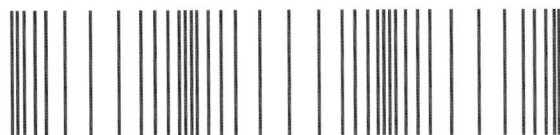

C a On the grid below, sketch a louder wave than the one shown.

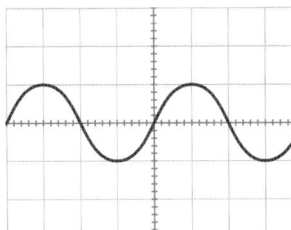

b The diagram shows a display of a sound wave on an screen.

    i Name the piece of apparatus used and explain how it is used
to measure the amplitude of the wave.

       _____

       _____

    ii If each vertical division represents 4 V, calculate the value of
the amplitude.

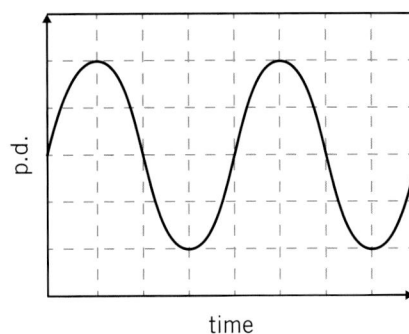

p.d.

time

_____

D When a neighbour is being noisy, sound waves transmit through the solid wall and into the air in your room. Describe
in detail what happens to the particles in the wall and air as a sound wave is transmitted from one to the other.

_____

_____

_____

_____

4.1.3 Frequency and pitch

A Fill in the gaps to complete the sentences.

A sound with high pitch has a high _____. This is measured in _____ (Hz). 1000 hertz

make up one _____ (kHz). Humans cannot hear sound waves with a _____ below

_____ Hz; these are called _____. Humans also cannot hear sound waves with

a _____ above _____ Hz; these are called _____. The range of

frequencies that a human can hear is called the _____ range.

B The diagram shows a sound wave on an oscilloscope.

    a Draw an arrow on this diagram and label it to show the time period.

    b The time base setting is 5 ms per division. Calculate the time period for this wave. Give your answer in seconds.

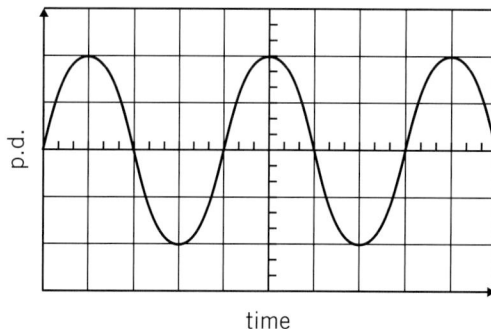

    c Calculate the frequency of the wave. The formula that relates frequency to time period is:

$$\text{frequency} = \frac{1}{\text{time period}}$$

C On the grid below, sketch a lower-pitched wave than the one shown.

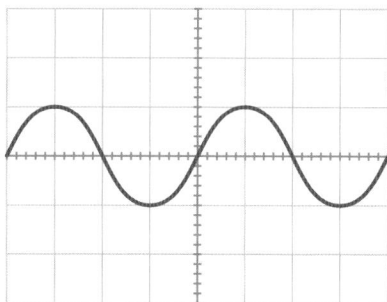

D The table shows the hearing range for several species, including humans.

Explain what each species would hear if there was a sound wave of 1000 Hz.

Species	Hearing range (Hz)	What will they hear for 1000 Hz sound wave?	Reason
Human	20–20 000		
Bat	2000–110 000		
Dog	67–45 000		

4.1.4 The ear and hearing

A Fill in the gaps to complete the sentences.

Your _____ detects sound waves by the outer ear or _____ collecting the waves and

directing them along the _____ canal to the middle ear where the _____ vibrates.

These vibrations pass to the _____, tiny bones that _____ the sound and

pass the vibration through the oval window to the inner ear or _____. Here the liquid and

_____ cells vibrate. Electrical signals are transmitted from here via the auditory _____

to the _____ and you hear the sound. Sound intensity, also called _____, is measured in

_____ (dB). Exposure to very loud sounds can permanently _____ the hair cells in the

cochlea so that you can become deaf.

B The statements below can be reordered to describe the process of you hearing someone speak. Read the statements and write down the order of statements you think will give the best description of this process.

Correct order ☐ ☐ ☐ ☐ ☐ ☐ ☐ ☐

1 pinna directs the sound wave

2 eardrum vibrates

3 sound wave travels through air

4 you hear the speech

5 vocal chords vibrate, creating a sound wave

6 ossicles amplify the sound

7 vibration reaches the cochlea

8 the signal travels down the auditory nerve

C Pneumatic drills are powerful drills used by road repair workers.

a Explain why ear defenders are used by workmen using a pneumatic drill. Include what happens if they do not wear ear defenders.

_____

_____

_____

b If the sound made by one drill is 10 dB more than the sound of another drill, proportionally how much louder is the first one than the second?

_____

D A company selling effective ear defenders has drafted an explanation of how their product works.

"The foam in our ear defenders transmits most of the sound wave. This ensures that the amplitude of the transmitted wave is large so that a lot of power reaches the user's ears."

Use your knowledge of sound waves to rewrite and correct this explanation.

_____

_____

_____

_____

4.2.1 Light

A Fill in the gaps to complete the sentences.

_____ objects emit light: they are a _____ of light. Most objects are _____ - _____ –

they do not emit light. You can see objects when light is _____ off them and absorbed by your

_____. Transparent substances _____ light. _____ substances do not.

_____ substances transmit light, but it is _____. If the Moon is between the _____

and the _____, a shadow called the _____ occurs on Earth, where the light from the Sun is totally

blocked and there will be a _____ _____ eclipse. The _____ occurs where only part of

the Sun's light is blocked and a _____ _____ eclipse occurs. If the Earth comes between the Sun

and the _____ and blocks the Sun's light from reaching the Moon, a _____ eclipse can occur.

B The statements below can be reordered to describe the process of seeing the Moon.
Read the statements and write down the order of statements that you think will give the best description.

Correct order: ☐ ☐ ☐ ☐ ☐

1 The Moon is a non-luminous object.
2 Some of the reflected light is absorbed in your eye.
3 It does not emit light itself, it just reflects light from the Sun.
4 The Sun is a luminous object.
5 It is a source of light – it emits light waves through space.

C The diagram shows the Sun, Moon, and Earth in the relative positions when a solar eclipse is visible.

An umbra is a shadow where a light source is entirely blocked. A penumbra is a shadow where part of a light source is blocked.

a Label where the two types of shadow, umbra and penumbra, lie on the Earth's surface.

b Explain where on the Earth's surface a partial eclipse is visible.

_____

_____

D There is a cat playing outside a window. You are looking at the cat in daylight.
Suggest how light interacts with each of the following.

a Cat _____

b Glass in window _____

c Back of your eye _____

4.2.2 Reflection

A Fill in the gaps to complete the sentences.

Light _____ off a mirror in the same way that a wave _____ off a barrier. The light

that hits the mirror is called the _____ ray. The reflected light is called the _____

ray. An imaginary line at 90° to the mirror is called the _____. You measure angles from the normal

to the rays of light. Rays reflect from surfaces with an angle of reflection _____ to the angle of

_____. This is called the law of _____. With a flat or _____ mirror, the

surface is smooth, causing _____ reflection; the reflected rays give a _____ image, as

if there is someone the same shape and size as you the other side of the mirror. With a rough surface, the light is

_____ – it bounces off in all directions. This is called _____ reflection where no image

is visible.

B **a** Write down how the angle of reflection relates to the angle of incidence.

_____

b The diagram on the right shows one form of reflection.
Does it show specular reflection or diffuse scattering? _____

c Explain how the law of reflection causes this form of reflection.

_____

_____

rough
surface

_____

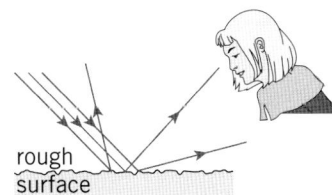

C Someone looks at the reflection of a candle in a plane mirror. Draw a ray diagram showing how an image is formed.

D Use the concepts of specular reflection and diffuse scattering to explain the following.

a On a sunny day, a room with windows appears bright inside even if you are not sitting in direct sunlight.

_____

_____

_____

b Sometimes outside on a sunny day you will see very bright bits of light when passing cars and the windows of
buildings.

_____

_____

_____

4.2.3 Refraction

A Fill in the gaps to complete the sentences.

When light passes from one _____ into another it changes _____. This causes

it to change _____; a process called _____. If light goes from air into glass it

_____ _____ and bends _____ the normal. This effect makes swimming

pools appear _____ than they are. Refraction is used in a convex or _____ lens to

_____ light on a focal point. Refraction is used in a concave or _____ lens to spread

light out.

B **a** If you are above a pond looking down at a stone, the stone appears to be nearer the surface than it really is. Explain why this happens.

_____

_____

_____

b Complete this ray diagram that illustrates the scenario described in part **a**, showing how the two rays refract to form an image.

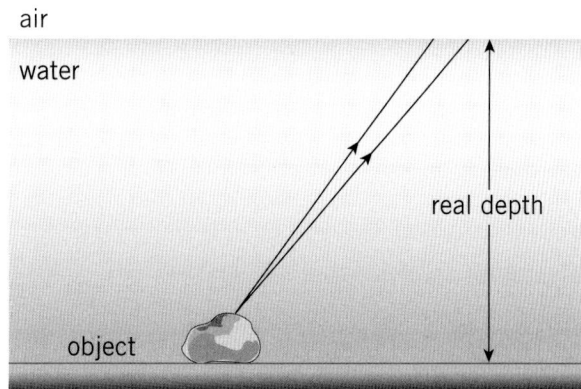

C **a** Draw a ray diagram to show how a converging lens forms an image.

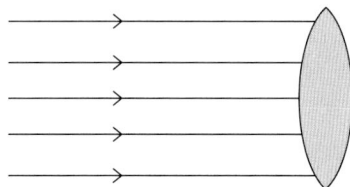

b Explain what happens when light travels through a converging lens so that an image is formed.

_____

_____

_____

4.2.4 The eye and vision

A Fill in the gaps to complete the sentences.

Your eye works by _____ light reflected from an _____ you are looking at. Your cornea

and _____ focus the light. Your _____ controls the size of your _____,

letting through more or less light. A real (not virtual) inverted image is formed on your _____ where

_____ absorb the light, causing _____ reactions which send electrical signals along

the _____ nerve to your brain.

B Draw a line to match each part in the left-hand column with its function.

object	A hole that allows light to enter the lens.
cornea and lens	Controls the size of the pupil, allowing in more or less light.
iris	Real (you could put a screen here and you would see an image), inverted, smaller than the object.
pupil	Where the image forms – contains photoreceptors.
retina	Reflected light from this enters the eye.
photoreceptors	Rods and cones – absorb light causing a chemical reaction which produces an electrical signal.
image	Sends electrical signal to the brain.
optic nerve	Focus the light.

C Explain how the eye forms an image. In your explanation, include whether the image is real or virtual, inverted or not, and larger or smaller than the object being viewed.

_____

_____

_____

D The diagram shows the eye of a short-sighted person.

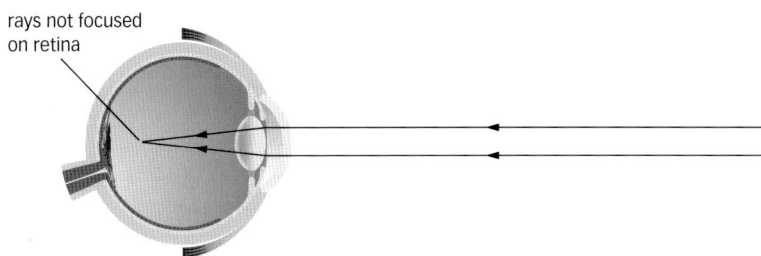

rays not focused
on retina

Explain the cause of short-sightedness and why a particular type of lens is used to correct this condition.

_____

_____

_____

_____

4.2.5 Colour

A Fill in the gaps to complete the sentences.

Our eyes detect three _____ colours of light: red, green, and blue. Two of these colours of light

added together make _____ colours of light, for instance blue and green light added together

make _____ light. All three _____ colours of light added together make

_____ light. Filters _____ light; for instance, a blue filter _____ all

colours except _____ from white light.

Coloured objects subtract light by _____ only their own colour. For example, a blue object appears

blue because when white light falls on it, all colours are absorbed except _____, which reflects.

A _____ can be used to split up light into a _____ of different colours. It does this

because of _____: light with the highest _____ (violet) refracts more than light with

the _____ frequency (red). The spectrum from the Sun's light is _____ – it has no gaps.

B Explain why a prism forms a spectrum.

_____

_____

_____

C Explain how primary colours are combined to form the secondary colour yellow.

_____

_____

_____

D **a** A white object is illuminated by red light and viewed through a green filter.

Suggest and explain how it will appear.

_____

_____

_____

b A green object is illuminated by white light and viewed through a green filter.

Suggest and explain how it will appear.

_____

_____

_____

E A red ball is illuminated using yellow light. Suggest and explain how it will appear.

_____

_____

_____

Big Idea 4 Pinchpoint ⊗

Pinchpoint question

Answer the question below, then do the follow-up activity **with the same letter** as the answer you picked.

A ray of light is travelling in glass.
Choose the ray diagram below that correctly shows what happens when the ray hits the edge of the glass.

A	B
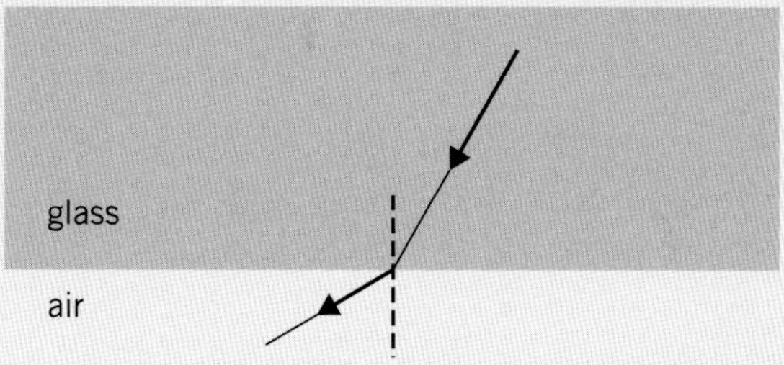 glass / air	glass / air

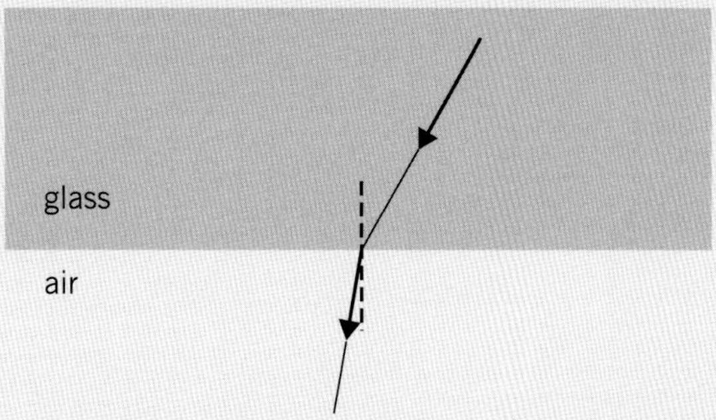

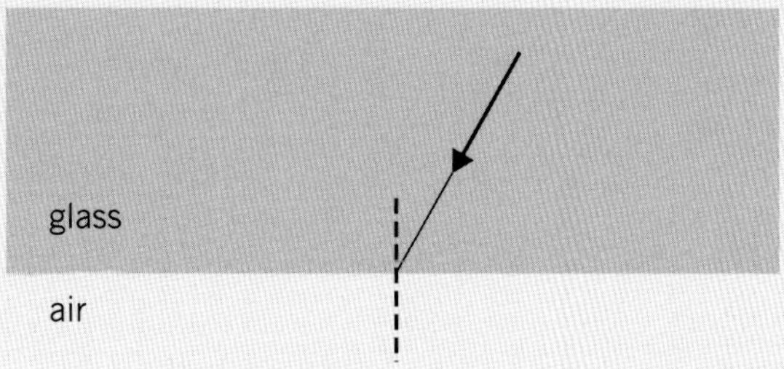

C	D
glass / air	glass / air

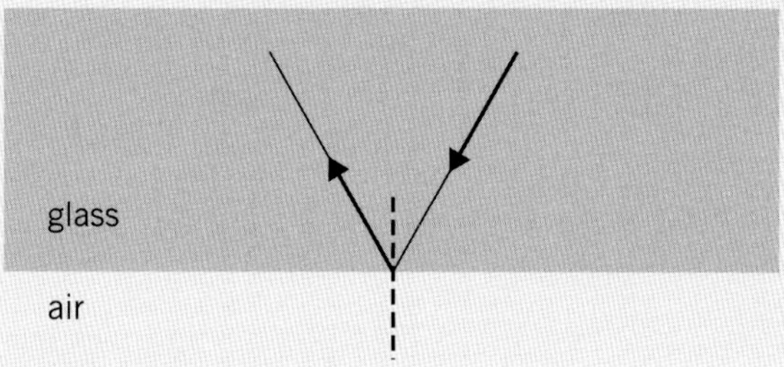

Follow-up activities

A a Does light travel faster or slower in glass compared to air? _____

b In your own words, write down the rules that light rays obey during refraction. Use each of the following keywords at least once.

medium	towards	away	normal	faster	slower	refracts

_____

_____

_____

Hint: Which way does light refract when moving from one transparent medium to another? For help see 4.2.3 Refraction.

B Use the concept of refraction to explain the appearance of this spoon through the water.

_____

_____

_____

_____

_____

_____

Hint: When will a light ray refract? For help see 4.2.3 Refraction.

C Complete the sentences using these keywords.

slower	absorbed	faster	slower	refract
normal	transmitted	faster		scattered

Light can interact with matter in different ways. It will be _____ in an opaque material. It will be

_____ in a translucent material. It will be _____ through a transparent material.

When passing from one transparent medium into another, the behaviour depends on the speed of light in those

materials. It will _____ towards the _____ going from a medium in which it is

_____ (such as air) into one where it is _____ (such as glass). It will refract away from

the normal going from a medium in which it is _____ into one where it is _____.

Hint: When will a light ray refract? For help see 4.2.3 Refraction.

D a Complete the following sentences using these keywords.

transmitted	speeds up	mirror	reflected
away from	refracts	towards	slows down

A _____ is a smooth sheet of metallic, opaque material (often behind a sheet of glass to protect

it). Light is _____ from mirrors; it is not _____. It _____ when it

passes from one transparent medium into another. When a light ray passes from air into glass, it will bend

_____ the normal as it _____. It will bend _____ the normal when

passing from water into air as it _____.

b Sketch below what happens when a ray of light in air:

i reaches a mirror.

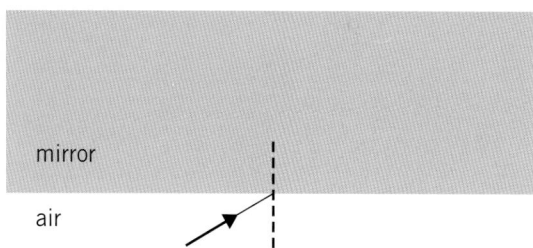

mirror

air

ii passes into glass.

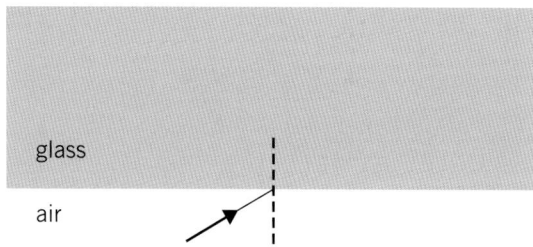

glass

air

Hint: When will a light ray refract? For help see 4.2.3 Refraction.

Pinchpoint review
Now look back at the question – do you think you chose the right letter?
Turn to the Answers page to find out.

Section 1 Revision questions

1 🧪🧪 A skydiver is falling to Earth with her parachute open.

   a Name a force acting on her which changes with distance. *(1 mark)*

   _____

   _____

   b Identify both forces for one interaction pair involving the skydiver and describe why they are an interaction pair. *(4 marks)*

   _____

   _____

   _____

   _____

   _____

   _____

2 🧪🧪 The speed of sound in air is 340 m/s and in water it is 1500 m/s.
Explain why these are different. *(2 marks)*

   _____

   _____

   _____

   _____

3 🧪🧪 Describe **two** ways that your hearing can be impaired. *(2 marks)*

   _____

   _____

   _____

   _____

4 🧪🧪 The lighting technician on a film set wants to produce different colours. He requires cyan but only has red, green, and blue lamps available.

   a Describe how he can produce the secondary colour cyan from the primary colours. *(2 marks)*

   _____

   b The film set has some coloured glass that acts as a green filter. The technician tests the coloured glass to see whether light will emerge from it for each primary lamp, and if so, what colour light it is. Complete **Table 1** to show his findings. *(3 marks)*

Table 1

Colour of lamp	Does light emerge from glass?	If yes, which colour?
red		
green		
blue		

5 🧪🧪 a Circle the quantity that flows in an electric circuit. *(1 mark)*

   resistance   potential difference

   charge   components

   b When a potential difference of 12 V is applied across a bulb, a current of 4.0 A flows through it. Calculate the resistance of the bulb. Give the unit.

   The formula for calculating resistance is:

   $$resistance = \frac{potential\,difference}{current}$$ *(2 marks)*

   _____

   c The wires leading into the bulb are wrapped with plastic with a resistance of 1 000 000 Ω. Circle whether the plastic wrapping and the filament wire are conductors or insulators.

   filament wire: **conductor / insulator** *(1 mark)*

   plastic wrapping: **conductor / insulator** *(1 mark)*

6 🧪🧪 An engineer is designing a machine to lift patients in a hospital.

   a The machine must increase the gravitational potential energy store for the patient by at least 1200 J in 20 s.

   Calculate the minimum power needed from the motor and include the unit for power. The formula for calculating power is:

   $$power = \frac{energy}{time}$$ *(2 marks)*

   _____

   b For convenience, the engineer decides to use a rechargeable battery. The hospital managers need to know how much it will cost to charge the battery. The battery recharges at 60 W for 2 hours, and the electricity company charges 15p per kW h.

i Convert 60 W to kW. *(1 mark)*

_____

ii Calculate the cost of charging the battery for 2 hours. Give your answer in pence. *(3 marks)*

_____

7 🧪🧪 **a** **Figure 1** shows a distance–time graph for one part of a journey.

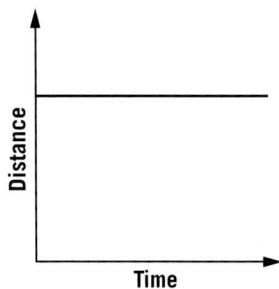

Figure 1

Describe what is happening. *(1 mark)*

_____ _____

b **Table 2** contains data for Clara walking to visit a friend.

Table 2

Time (s)	Distance (m)
0	0
120	180
180	180
300	280

Draw a distance–time graph for this journey. *(3 marks)*

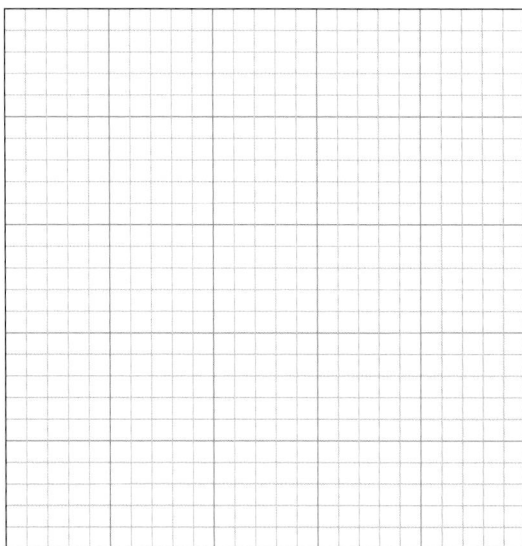

c Calculate the speed of the first part of Clara's journey. *(3 marks)*

_____

8 🧪🧪 In 2006, Hannah McKeand set the record for reaching the South Pole in the fastest time by foot.

On her trip, McKeand needed to absorb 3000 kJ of energy from her food each hour. While working in an office, a typical adult would need to consume 400 kJ of energy in her food every hour.

Is McKeand's energy intake larger or smaller than that of an office worker? Suggest why. *(2 marks)*

_____

_____

9 🧪🧪 **a** Describe an example of light being refracted, including what happens to the ray of light. *(2 marks)*

_____

_____

b Explain why light is refracted in the example you gave in part **a**. *(1 mark)*

_____

_____

c Complete the ray diagram in **Figure 2** to show what happens when light travels through a converging lens. *(2 marks)*

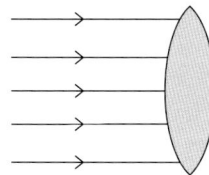

Figure 2

d A physicist learnt about a property of lenses called 'power'. You need a more 'powerful' or stronger spectacle lens if your eyesight is poor. She measured the focal length of lenses of different powers and drew this graph.

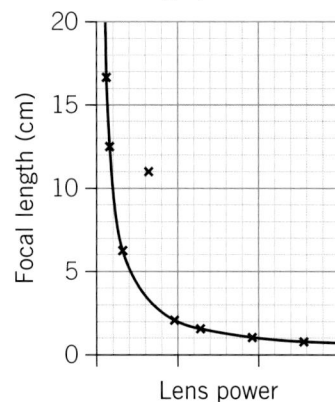

Describe any pattern and any anomalies in this graph.
(3 marks)

_____

_____

_____

10 ⚗️⚗️⚗️ Voyager 1 is the space probe that has travelled furthest from Earth; it is currently leaving the Solar System.

  a Explain how the effect of gravity on its mass and weight has changed as it has moved away from Earth.
(3 marks)

_____

_____

_____

  b **Table 3** shows data that were gathered for a test rocket.

Table 3

Force (kN)	Acceleration (m/s^2)
1	14
2	30
3	46
4	59
5	72

Plot a graph of acceleration against force and draw a line of best fit.
(3 marks)

11 ⚗️⚗️⚗️ On the axes below, sketch two waves of different loudness but the same pitch. Label them to indicate which is louder.
(3 marks)

12 ⚗️⚗️⚗️ Some sunlight falls at an angle on two different objects: a transparent window made of glass, and an opaque blue ball. Predict how light will interact with these two objects.
(4 marks)

_____

_____

_____

_____

_____

_____

13 ⚗️⚗️⚗️ You are a scientific adviser to the British Government. They have asked for advice on future electricity generation.

Discuss the advantages and disadvantages of the two energy resources shown in **Table 4**.
(6 marks)

Table 4

Energy resource	Estimated cost per unit of electricity in 2015 (£ / MW h)
Natural gas	74
Onshore wind	89

_____

_____

_____

_____

_____

14 🧪🧪🧪 Ezra has a 1500W kettle and is deciding whether to buy a new 3000W kettle.

a Using the information in **Table 5**, predict and explain whether Ezra's electricity bill is likely to increase, decrease, or stay the same. *(4 marks)*

Table 5

Kettle power (W)	Time to boil 1 kg of water (s)
1500	300
3000	140

_____

_____

_____

_____

_____

b Ezra would like to know which kettle is best. Suggest whether this is a question that can be investigated scientifically as it is, and give a reason. *(2 marks)*

_____

_____

_____

_____

15 🧪🧪🧪 Abi starts working in a new office and notices that she often gets an electric shock when she touches the metal door handle. She notices that there is a different kind of carpet from where she worked before.

a Explain why Abi receives a shock when touching the door handle. *(1 mark)*

_____

_____

_____

_____

_____

_____

b Charlotte works in a different building and wants to investigate this effect. She finds that she does not receive a shock in any of the rooms of the other building.

Suggest **one** reason why not. *(1 mark)*

_____

_____

Section 1 Checklist

Revision question number	Outcome	Topic reference	☹	☺	☻
1a	Describe simply how gravity varies with mass and distance.	1.2.1			
1b	Identify interaction pairs in a simple situation.	1.1.1			
2	Explain observations where sound is transmitted by different media.	4.1.1			
3	Describe how your hearing can be damaged.	4.1.4			
4a	Describe how primary colours add to make secondary colours.	4.2.5			
4b	Predict the colour of objects in red light and the colour of light through different filters.	4.2.5			
5a	State what current is.	2.2.1			
5b	Calculate resistance of a circuit.	2.1.2			
5c	Describe the difference between conductors and insulators in terms of resistance	2.1.2			
6	Predict the power requirements of different home devices, and compare their energy usage and how much they cost to run.	3.1.3			
7	Interpret distance–time graphs.	1.1.4			
8	Compare the energy in food and fuels with the energy needed for different activities.	3.1.1			
9a, b	Describe what happens when light is refracted.	4.2.3			
9c	Use a ray diagram to describe what happens when light travels through a convex or concave lens.	4.2.3			
9d	Analyse data from an investigation to draw up a detailed conclusion, describe relationships, and suggest alternative explanations where appropriate.	EP4			
10a	Explain how the effect of gravity changes moving away from Earth, and in keeping objects in orbit.	1.2.1			
10b	Plot data on a graph and draw the line of best fit.	EP4			
11	Compare and contrast waves of different loudness using a diagram.	4.1.2			
12	Predict how light will interact with different materials.	4.2.1			
13	Compare renewable and non-renewable resources.	3.1.2			
14a	Predict the effect on energy bills of changing the power of equipment.	3.1.3			
14b	Explain how and why some questions can be investigated and why some cannot.	EP1			
15a	Explain, in terms of electrons, why something becomes charged.	2.2.2			
15b	Compare and contrast data, suggesting reasons why the data may be different.	EP5			

5.1.1 The particle model

A Fill in the gaps to complete the sentences.

Materials are made up of tiny _____. Many materials are mixtures of different substances. Different

substances are made from _____ particles. The properties of a substance describe what it

_____ like and how it _____. Every substance has its own properties, such as density.

The properties of a substance depend on what its particles are like, how its particles are _____, and

how its particles _____ around.

B a The table gives some information about particles in four substances. The diagrams show how the particles are arranged in solid gold and silver.

Substance	Radius of particle (nm)	Relative mass of particle
gold	0.144	197
hafnium	0.157	178
silver	0.144	108
zirconium	0.157	91

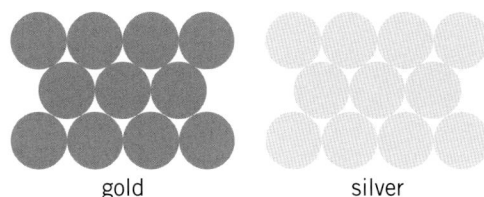

gold   silver

Choose data from the table to explain why gold has a greater density than silver. You will need to refer to the diagrams in your answer.

_____

_____

_____

_____

b The particle arrangements in solid hafnium and solid zirconium are the same as each other.

Choose data from the table in part **a** to predict which has the greater density.
Underline your answer: **hafnium / zirconium**

C A student uses spheres to model liquid gold and liquid silver. The diagrams show her models.
Evaluate how the student's model:

a helps to explain why you can pour liquid gold.

_____

_____

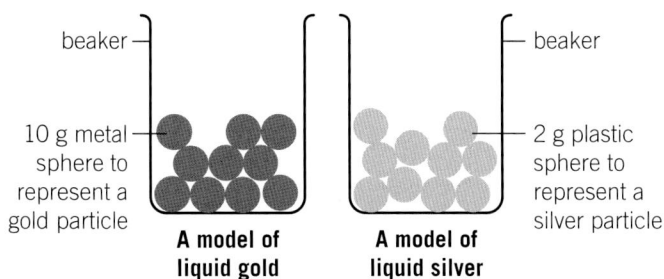

beaker

10 g metal sphere to represent a gold particle

A model of liquid gold

beaker

2 g plastic sphere to represent a silver particle

A model of liquid silver

b helps to explain why 1 cm³ of gold has a greater mass than 1 cm³ of silver.

_____

_____

c helps to show that every substance has different particles.

_____

_____

d is different from real liquid gold and real liquid silver.

_____

5.1.2 States of matter

A Fill in the gaps to complete the sentences.

Most substances can exist in the solid state, the liquid state, and the _____ state. These are the three

states of _____. The particles of a substance in each of its three states are the same. In each of the

three states of matter, the arrangement and _____ of the particles are _____.

B Tick one or more columns next to each property to show the possible state or states of the substance.

Property of substance	The substance could be in the ...		
	solid state	liquid state	gas state
Can be compressed			
Can be poured			
Has a fixed shape			
Has fixed volume			

C Use the particle model to explain each observation below. Each explanation should be one short sentence only.

a A solid has a fixed shape.

_____

b A liquid cannot be compressed.

_____

c A gas flows.

_____

D James drew the diagram shown to represent a substance in the liquid state.
Evaluate his drawing.

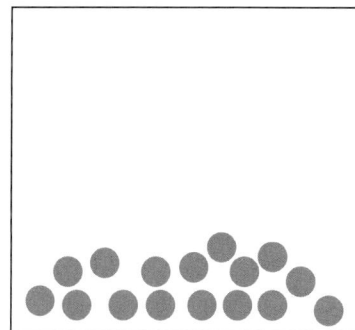

_____

_____

_____

_____

_____

E Two students are talking about sand.

You can pour sand, so it is liquid.

Hannah

You cannot compress sand, so it is solid.

Brooke

a Write down the name of the student who is correct. _____

b Explain why the other student is incorrect.

_____

_____

5.1.3 Melting and freezing

A Fill in the gaps to complete the sentences.

The change of state from solid to liquid is called _____. When a solid warms up, its particles vibrate

_____. The solid melts when its particles move _____ from their places in the

pattern. A substance melts at its _____ point. A _____ substance has a sharp

melting point. The change of state from a liquid to a solid is called _____. When a liquid cools, its

particles move around more _____. It freezes when its particles get into a regular pattern and

vibrate in fixed positions.

B Box **1** shows some particles in a liquid.

    a Draw the same number of particles in box **2** to show how the particles might be arranged when the liquid in box **1** has frozen.

    b Describe how the particle movement and energy changes when a liquid freezes.

Box 1   Box 2

_____

_____

_____

_____

C Rashid has a hot liquid. He measures the temperature every minute as the liquid cools. His data are in the table.

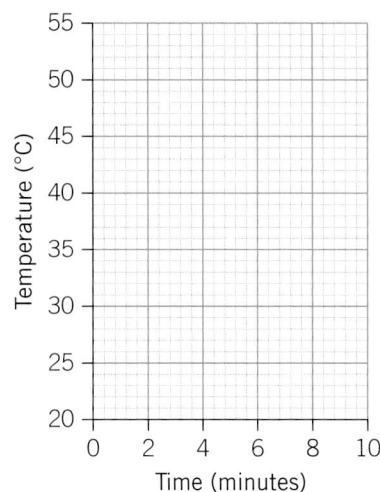

Time (min)	Temperature (°C)	Time (min)	Temperature (°C)
0	50	6	35
1	45	7	35
2	38	8	35
3	35	9	32
4	35	10	25
5	35		

Copy the axes on the right, and plot a graph to show the data in the table.
Then label the graph to show where the following statements are true.

- This is the melting point of the substance.
- The solid is cooling down.
- The particles are moving around more and more slowly.
- The particles are arranging themselves in a pattern.
- All the particles are vibrating about fixed points.
- Some of the particles are moving around and some are vibrating about fixed points.

A Fill in the gaps to complete the sentences.

A substance can change from the liquid to the _____ state by boiling. Boiling happens when

bubbles of the substance in the _____ state form everywhere in the liquid and rise to the surface to

escape into the air. The total mass of the gas and _____ is the same as the mass of the liquid at the

start. Scientists say the mass is _____ in boiling. A substance boils at a certain temperature and this is

called its _____ point.

B The table gives some data for four substances.

Substance	Melting point (°C)	Boiling point (°C)
bromine	−7	59
mercury	−39	357
xenon	−112	−108

Complete the sentences below by writing the name of the substance being described. Use only the **boiling point** data to help you.

The substance with the lowest boiling point is _____. The substance with the strongest attractive forces

between particles in the liquid is _____. The substance that needs most energy to change an amount

containing 1 million particles from liquid to gas is _____.

C Draw a line to match each substance to its state at the given temperature. You will need to use **melting point data** and **boiling point data** from the table in activity **B**.

bromine at 20 °C   solid

mercury at 400 °C   liquid

xenon at −115 °C   gas

D A student heats a liquid. The graph shows how its temperature changes with time.

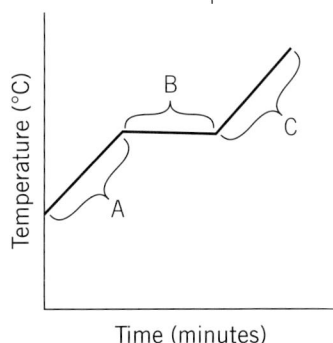

The letters A, B, and C show different periods during the heating. Write **one**, **two**, or **three** letters next to each statement. You can use each letter once or more than once.

a In these periods, energy is transferred from the surroundings to the substance. _____

b In these periods, the particles move faster as temperature increases. _____

c In this period, the energy transferred is separating particles from each other to make bubbles of

gas. _____

d In this period, the energy transferred is making bubbles of gas escape from the liquid. _____

5.1.5 More changes of state

A Fill in the gaps to complete the sentences.

A substance can change from the liquid to the _____ state by evaporation or boiling. Evaporation

happens when particles leave the _____ of a liquid. The change of state from gas to liquid is called

_____. The change of state from solid to gas is called _____.

B A student investigates how quickly drops of water evaporate in different places. He sets up the apparatus shown.

drop of water   Petri dish

The student puts each Petri dish in a different place: one on top of a heater, one in a fridge, and one on a windowsill. He measures the time taken for all the water to evaporate from each dish.

a Complete the table with the names of the variables in the experiment.

Type of variable	Variable
independent	
dependent	
control	

b Explain why it is important to keep constant the control variable you identified in part **a**.

_____

C The statements below describe the arrangement and movement of particles in different states, and during changes of state.

1 The particles are arranged in a regular pattern. They vibrate on the spot.

2 The particles are spread out. They move around randomly.

3 The particles are arranged randomly, touching their neighbours. They move from place to place, sliding over each other.

4 More and more particles leave the liquid surface.

5 Some particles leave their place in the regular pattern. They move far away from their neighbours.

6 The particles move closer together.

7 Bubbles form everywhere in the liquid. In the bubbles, the particles are spread out.

8 Some particles, with more energy than the others, leave the liquid surface.

9 Bubbles rise to the surface and their particles leave the liquid.

Write down, **in the correct order**:

a The letters of three statements that explain what happens to particles during sublimation.

_____

b The letters of three statements that explain what happens to particles during condensation.

_____

c The letters of four statements that explain what happens to particles during evaporation.

_____

d The letters of four statements that explain what happens to particles during boiling.

_____

5.1.6 Diffusion

A Fill in the gaps to complete the sentences.

The random movement and _____ of particles is called diffusion. Diffusion happens in the liquid

and _____ states because the particles in these states move around all the time. An example of

_____ is when a drop of ink spreads through water. The particles move by themselves. You do not

need to shake or _____.

B Edward puts some flowers in the corner of a room.
Half an hour later, he can smell the flowers wherever he is in the room.

  a Add some particles to the diagram to show why he can smell the flowers everywhere in the room.

    Draw each particle as a small circle.

  b Explain why the particles you drew in part **a** have diffused.

    _____

C A student investigates the diffusion of purple potassium manganate(VII) when it dissolves in water. She wants to find out how temperature affects the time for the purple colour to spread out. She sets up this apparatus.

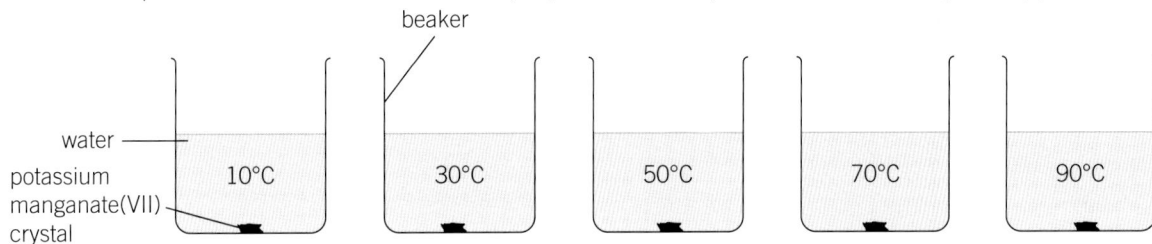

beaker

water

potassium manganate(VII) crystal

10°C   30°C   50°C   70°C   90°C

  a Complete the table to identify the different types of variable in the investigation.

Variable	Type of variable
Time for the purple colour to spread out	
Size of crystals	
Temperature of water	
Volume of water	

  b Explain why there will be uncertainty in the measurement of the dependent variable.

    _____

  c Explain why one of the control variables is not easy to control.

    _____

  d Predict what the results of the investigation will show.

    _____

  e Use the particle model to explain your prediction.

    _____

5.1.7 Gas pressure

A Fill in the gaps to complete the sentences.

The particles in a gas move randomly in _____ directions. When they move, they may hit – or

_____ with – the walls of the container. The collisions exert a _____ on the walls.

The force per unit area acting on a surface is the gas _____.

B Catherine is at the bottom of a mountain. She allows air to fill a glass jar (jar **X**) and screws on the lid. At the top of the mountain she allows air to fill another glass jar (jar **Y**). The diagrams show the particles in the jars.

Use particle theory to explain why the gas pressure in jar **Y** is less than the gas pressure in jar **X**, if both jars are at the same temperature.

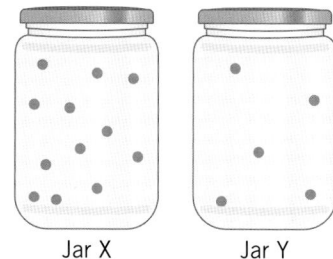

Jar X   Jar Y

_____

_____

C Look at the diagrams in activity **B**. Tick the statements below to show whether they are true or false, or whether it is not possible to know.

Statement	✓ if it is definitely true	✓ if it is definitely false	✓ if it is not possible to know whether it is true or false
If the temperature in jar **X** increases, the pressure increases.			
If the temperature in jar **Y** increases, the pressure in jar **Y** will be greater than the pressure in jar **X**.			
If more particles are added to jar **Y**, the pressure will increase.			
If some particles are removed from jar **X**, the pressure in jar **X** will be less than the pressure in jar **Y**.			
If more particles are added to jar **X**, the pressure will decrease.			
If the temperature in jar **X** increases, the pressure in jar **X** will be greater than the pressure in jar **Y**.			

D Josh blows up a balloon. He uses a tape measure the find the distance around the balloon. Then Josh puts the balloon in the freezer. Half an hour later, he measures the distance around the balloon again, and finds that it is smaller.

Use the particle model to explain why the balloon gets smaller in the freezer.

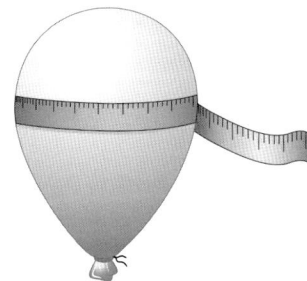

_____

_____

_____

5.1.8 Inside particles

A Fill in the gaps to complete the sentences.

A substance is made up of _____ type of material only. There are two types of substances – elements

and _____. An element is a substance that _____ be broken down into other

substances, and that contains _____ type of atom. A compound is a substance made up of atoms

of _____ or more elements, _____ joined together. The smallest part of an element

that can exist is called an _____. A particle that is made up of two or more atoms, strongly joined

together, is called a _____.

B Zinc and sulfur are elements. Zinc sulfide is a compound of zinc and sulfur.

Tick the statements below that are true.

1 All the atoms in a piece of sulfur are the same. ☐

2 Zinc atoms are the same as sulfur atoms. ☐

3 Zinc sulfide is made up of one type of atom. ☐

4 The atoms in zinc gas are far apart, but the atoms in solid sulfur are closely packed together. ☐

C The diagrams show particles of six different substances. Write the letters of the correct diagrams next to the statements below.

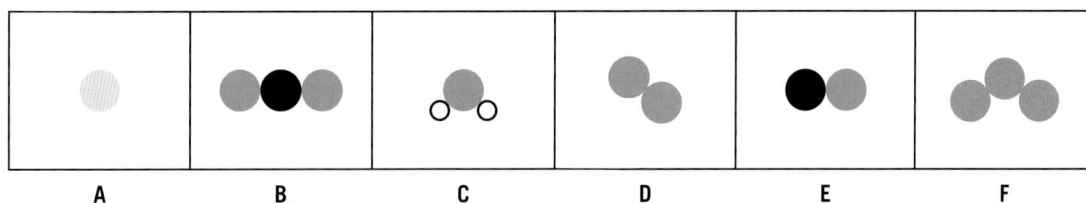

| A | B | C | D | E | F |

a Which **three** diagrams show elements? _____, _____ and _____

b Which diagram shows an element that exists as single atoms? _____

c Which **two** diagrams show elements that exist as molecules? _____ and _____

d Which **three** diagrams show compounds? _____ _____ and _____

e Which **two** diagrams show different forms of the same element? _____ and _____

f Which **two** diagrams show two different compounds that are both made up of atoms of the same two elements? _____ and _____

D In each box at the bottom of the page, draw one diagram to show the atoms in one molecule of each substance in the list below.

Represent each atom with a circle. Use these colours:

- oxygen atom – red
- carbon atom – black
- hydrogen atom – white
- nitrogen atom – blue

a A hydrogen molecule, made up of two hydrogen atoms.

b A water molecule, made up of one oxygen atom (in the middle) joined to two hydrogen atoms.

c A methane molecule, made up of one carbon atom (in the middle) joined to four hydrogen atoms.

d A nitrogen monoxide molecule, made up of one nitrogen atom joined to one oxygen atom.

e A nitrogen dioxide molecule, made up of one nitrogen atom (in the middle) joined to two oxygen atoms.

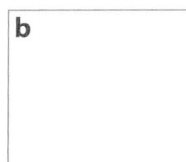

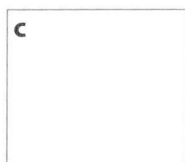

a	b	c	d	e

5.2.1 Pure substances and mixtures

A Fill in the gaps to complete the sentences.

If a substance does not have other substances mixed with it, it is _____ and has a

_____ melting point. If a substance has other substances mixed with it, it is _____

and melts over a range of _____. A mixture contains _____ than one substance.

Its different substances are _____ joined together. You can change the amounts of the different

substances in a _____, and the substances in a mixture keep their own _____.

B A student measures the melting temperatures of four substances: **W**, **X**, **Y**, and **Z**.
Her results are in the table.

Substance	Temperature the substance started to melt at (°C)	Temperature that the mixture finished melting at (°C)
W	11	13
X	51	51
Y	37	53
Z	79	79

Write down the letters of the **two** pure substances in the table, and explain how you decided.

Pure substances: _____ and _____

Reason for decision: _____   _____

C The diagrams below show some pure substances, and some mixtures, all in the gas state.
Each circle represents one atom. Different colour circles represent atoms of different elements.

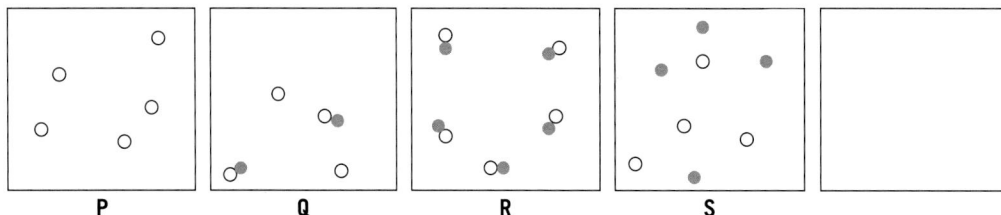

P   Q   R   S

a Write down the letter of the correct diagram next to each description below.

i A mixture of elements _____

ii A pure element _____

iii A pure compound _____

iv A mixture of an element and a compound _____

b In the empty box, draw a diagram to show some particles in a mixture of two different compounds.

Hint: In a compound, each particle is made up of atoms of more than one element.

D Complete the table to describe how to separate each mixture, and why your chosen method works.

Mixture	How to separate the mixture	Why this method works
Sand and water		
Sand and steel nails		
Flour and marbles		

Hint: To help you to explain why each method works, think about the properties of the substances in the mixture.

5.2.2 Solutions

A Fill in the gaps to complete the sentences.

When you mix sugar with water, the sugar dissolves to make a _____. Sugar is the

_____ and water is the _____. In a solution, several solvent particles surround each

_____ particle. The particles _____ around. In a solution, you _____ see

two separate substances, and all parts of the mixture are the _____. In a solution, the solvent is in the

_____ state and the substance that dissolves in it can be in the solid or _____ state.

B For each pair of key words below, write one sentence about sugar and water. The sentence must include the two key words given, but none of the other key words.

For example: solvent, solution – In a solution of sugar in water, water is the solvent.

a solvents, dissolves _____

b solute, solvent _____

c dissolves, solution _____

C **a** In the box, draw and label a diagram showing some sugar and water particles in sugar solution. Use different coloured circles to show the sugar and water particles. Sugar particles are bigger than water particles.

b Describe what happens to the particles when sugar is added to water to make a solution.

_____

D **a** Ophelia dissolves 12 g of paracetamol in 1000 g of water. What mass of solution does she make?

_____

b Marcus has 156 g of salt solution. He heats the solution and the water evaporates.
The mass of salt that remains is 7 g.
What mass of solvent was present in the original solution?

_____

c Normal saline solution is used in hospital drips. The solution usually contains 9.0 g of salt dissolved in 1004.6 g of solution.
Calculate the mass of water in 1004.6 g of the saline solution.

_____

E **a** Nail polish remover is mainly propanone.
Suggest why propanone can remove nail polish, but water cannot.

_____

b A can of fizzy drink has four main ingredients – water, carbon dioxide, sugar, and flavourings.
Name the solvent and solutes in the drink.

Solvent _____

Solutes _____, _____, and _____

5.2.3 Solubility

A Fill in the gaps to complete the sentences.

A solution in which no more solute can dissolve is called a _____ solution. The mass of solute that

dissolves in 100 g of water to make a saturated solution is the _____ of the solute. If a substance

dissolves in a solvent, scientists say that the substance is _____. The greater the mass of solute that

can dissolve, the more _____ the solute.

B **a** The statements below can be reordered to describe an experiment to investigate the solubility of a solute at different temperatures. Read the statements and write down the order of statements you think will give the best method.

Correct order ☐ ☐ ☐ ☐ ☐

  1 Heat up some water in a kettle, and repeat the whole experiment four more times at different temperatures.

  2 Continue to add more and more solute to the water, with stirring, until no more dissolves.

  3 At room temperature, weigh out 100 g of water in a beaker.

  4 Use a spatula to add some solute to the water, and stir with a stirring rod.

  5 Record the final mass of the solution.

 b Describe how to calculate the mass of solute that dissolves in the experiment in part **a**.

  _____

 c Write down one **control variable** in the investigation in part **a** and explain why this variable must be controlled.
  Variable _____

  Reason the variable must be controlled _____

C The graph below shows the solubility of lead nitrate, and of potassium nitrate, at different temperatures.

 a Draw a line of best fit on the graph for the solubility of lead nitrate.

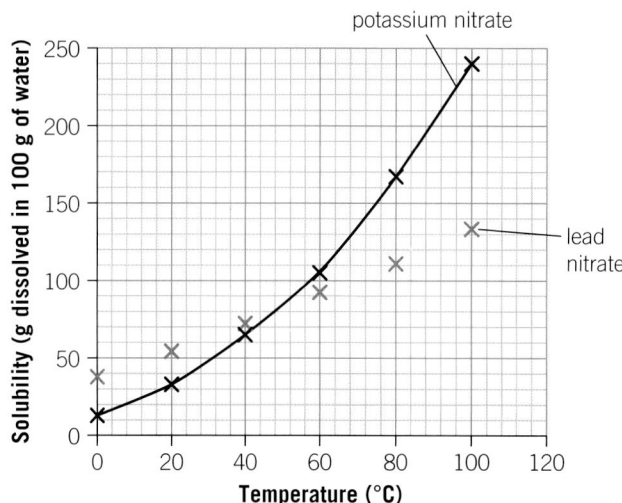

 b Tick the statements below that are true.

  1 At all temperatures, lead nitrate is more soluble than potassium nitrate. ☐

  2 At 80 °C, the mass of potassium nitrate that dissolves in 100 g of water is approximately 55 g more than the mass of lead nitrate that dissolves in 100 g of water. ☐

  3 Lead nitrate is more soluble than potassium nitrate below 50 °C, but potassium nitrate is more soluble than lead nitrate above 50 °C. ☐

  4 The solubility of lead nitrate is approximately 110 g/1000 g of water at 60 °C. ☐

5.2.4 Filtration

A Fill in the gaps to complete the sentences.

A mixture can be separated because the substances that are in it have _____ physical properties.

The method used to separate a mixture depends on which _____ properties are different.

Filtration, also called _____, separates a liquid from an _____ solid. It can also

separate excess solid that has not _____ in a solution. When you pour the mixture into filter paper,

the _____ or solution goes through tiny holes in the filter paper. The liquid or solution is the

_____. The solid remains in the filter paper cone. This is the _____.

B The statements below can be reordered to explain how filtration works. Read the statements and write down the order of statements you think will give the best explanation.

Correct order ☐ ☐ ☐ ☐ ☐

1 so they stay in the filter paper.

2 Water particles are smaller than the tiny holes,

3 Filter paper has tiny holes in it.

4 Grains of sand are bigger than the tiny holes,

5 so they pass through the filter paper.

C **a** Tick the mixtures in the table that can be separated by filtration.
For the mixtures that can be separated, write down the names of the residue and filtrate.

	Mixture	✔ if separable by filtration	Residue	Filtrate
1	Pieces of dirt from oil in a car engine			
2	Undissolved potassium chloride from a saturated solution of potassium chloride			
3	Coffee solution from ground-up coffee beans			
4	Potassium chloride from a dilute solution of potassium chloride			

b Choose **one** mixture in the table above that **can** be separated by filtration.
Explain why this mixture can be separated by filtration.

_____

_____

D A student makes a model to explain filtering. In her model, she uses:

- a sieve to represent filter paper
- marbles to represent sand
- flour to represent water

a Explain **one** way that the model is useful in explaining filtering.

_____

_____

b Explain **one** way that the model is **not** useful in explaining filtering.

_____

_____

E Look back at the solubility curve for potassium nitrate in 5.2.3.
A student makes a saturated solution by dissolving potassium nitrate in 100 g of water at 80 °C. She removes the undissolved potassium nitrate. Then the student cools the solution to 20 °C. She filters the mixture.
What is the maximum mass of solid potassium nitrate she can collect as residue?

maximum mass of solid potassium nitrate = _____ g

5.2.5 Evaporation and distillation

A Fill in the gaps to complete the sentences.

To obtain salt from salty water, you can use _____. The water evaporates, and salt (in the

_____ state) remains. Evaporation is used to obtain any _____ from its solution.

To obtain water from salty water, you need to use _____. Distillation uses evaporation and

_____ to obtain a solvent from its _____.

B Mr Ward showed his class how to use distillation to obtain pure water from salty water.
Add the numbers of the labels below to the diagram to explain how distillation works.

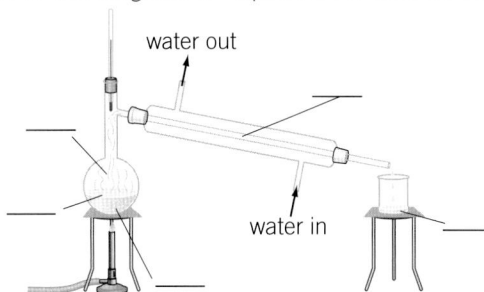

1 Water vapour condenses here.   **2** Pure liquid water.   **3** Water leaves the solution here, as a gas.

4 The volume of this solution gets less.   **5** This part of the apparatus is full of steam.

C Distillation and evaporation are both used to separate mixtures.

   a Tick **one** or **two** boxes next to each statement to show whether the statement is true for distillation, evaporation, or both.

	Statement	✔ true for evaporation	✔ true for distillation
1	The solvent changes state from liquid to gas.		
2	The purpose of the technique is to obtain a substance in the solid state.		
3	The solute remains in the container that is heated.		
4	The solvent evaporates, condenses, and is collected.		
5	The technique only works if the boiling points of the two substances in the mixture are different.		

   b Write two sentences to compare distillation and evaporation.

_____

_____

_____

Hint: In your answer, write one sentence about how the processes are similar, and one sentence about how the processes are different.

D Jasmine has some copper chloride solution. The solvent in the solution is water.

   a Name the one substance that Jasmine can obtain from this solution by distillation.

_____

   b Explain why Jasmine can use distillation, but not evaporation, to obtain this substance from the solution.

_____

_____

_____

5.2.6 Chromatography

A Fill in the gaps to complete the sentences.

The dyes that are mixed together in ink are soluble in the same _____. This means that you can

separate them by _____. In this process, the different dyes travel _____ distances up

the paper. This separates the dyes, which each make a separate _____ on the chromatogram.

B Sam grinds up some leaves with a solvent, and puts a spot of the juice on a piece of chromatography paper. On the same paper, he also puts spots of three other pigments (colours) that he thinks might be in the leaves. These are his reference spots.

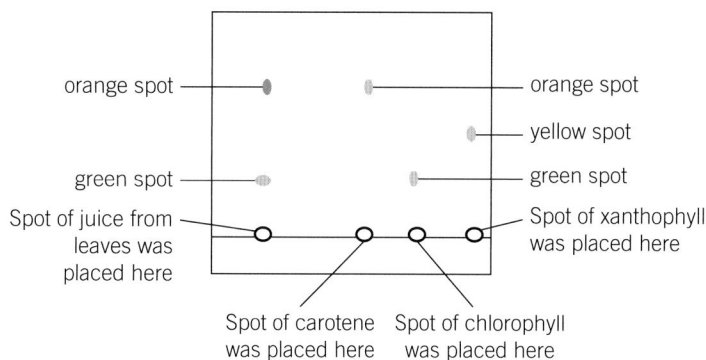

Here is Sam's chromatogram.

orange spot

green spot

Spot of juice from leaves was placed here

orange spot

yellow spot

green spot

Spot of xanthophyll was placed here

Spot of carotene was placed here

Spot of chlorophyll was placed here

a How many pigments are in the leaves?

_____

b Name one physical property that must be the same for each pigment in the leaves. _____

c Name one property that must be different for each pigment in the leaves. _____

d Name the two pigments that are probably in the leaves.

_____ and _____

e Explain why you cannot be certain that the pigments you named in part **b** are in the leaves.

_____

C Zoe wants to use chromatography to determine whether two reactants have finished reacting.

She starts by making a reference chromatogram. She carries out a chromatography experiment with the two reactants and the product of the chemical reaction (chromatogram **A**).

She then carries out the chemical reaction. After a few minutes she takes out a small sample of the reaction mixture, and makes chromatogram **B**.

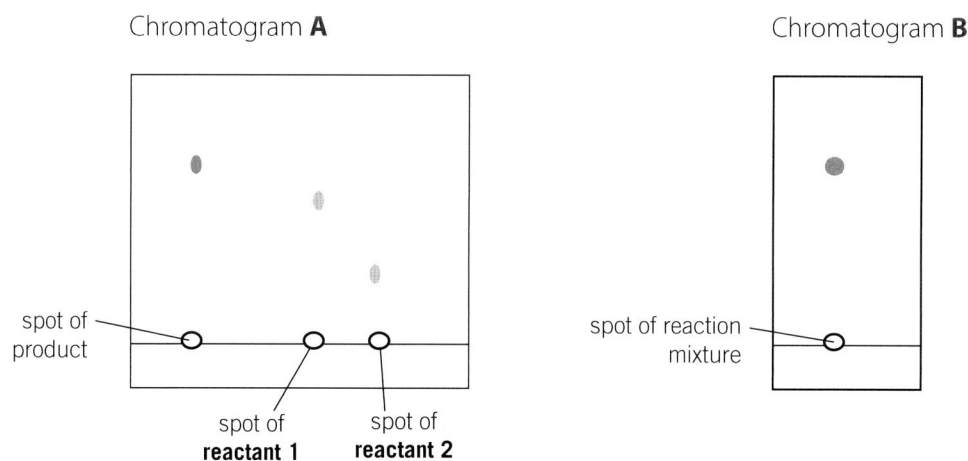

Chromatogram **A**

spot of product

spot of reactant 1

spot of reactant 2

Chromatogram **B**

spot of reaction mixture

Use information from both chromatograms to explain whether or not the reactants have finished reacting.

_____

_____

Pinchpoint question

Answer the question below, then do the follow-up activity **with the same letter** as the answer you picked.

The melting point of oxygen is −218 °C and its boiling point is −183 °C.

How are its particles arranged, and how do they move, at −200 °C?

A The particles are arranged randomly. They are close to their neighbours, but do not touch them. They move around randomly, sliding over each other.

B The particles are arranged randomly. They are far apart from each other. They move around randomly, throughout the container.

C The particles are arranged randomly. They touch their neighbours. They move around randomly, sliding over each other.

D The particles are arranged in a pattern. They are far apart from each other. They vibrate on the spot.

Follow-up activities

A Keira draws some particles in liquid water.

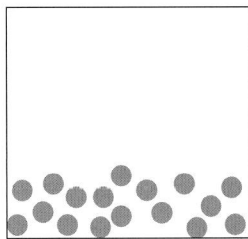

   a **i** Write down **two** things that she has drawn correctly in her drawing.

     1 _____

     2 _____

   ii Write down **one** thing that she has drawn incorrectly. _____

   b In the box, draw the correct arrangement of particles in liquid water.

Hint: How close together are the particles in a liquid? For help see 5.1.2 States of matter.

B Complete the table to give the state of each substance at **−100 °C**.

Substance	Melting point (°C)	Boiling point (°C)	State at −100 °C
argon	−189	−186	
chlorine	−101	−35	
mercury	−39	357	
xenon	−112	−108	
ytterbium	824	1430	
zirconium	1850	3580	

Hint: Sketch a temperature scale for the first substance, and label the melting point and boiling point. Then use the scale to work out the state of this substance at −100 °C. Repeat for the other substances. For help, see 5.1.4 Boiling.

C The melting point of bromine is −7 °C and its boiling point is 59 °C.

Draw a line to match each temperature to the correct description of the arrangement and to the correct description of movement of bromine particles at that temperature. Use each 'particle arrangement' and 'particle movement' statement once, more than once, or not at all.

Temperature (°C)	Particle arrangement	Particle movement
58		
	regular pattern	random, throughout the container
−5		
	random and touching	random, sliding over each other
60		
	random and far apart	vibrating on the spot
−10		

Hint: Start by using the melting and boiling point data to work out the state of bromine at each temperature. Then draw a line to match each state to the correct description of the particle arrangement and movement. For help see 5.1.2 States of matter, 5.1.3 Melting and freezing, and 5.1.4 Boiling.

D a Draw one diagram in each box below to show particles of a substance in the solid, liquid, and gas states.

solid

liquid

gas

b Complete the sentences below to describe how the particles are moving in each state.

In the solid state, the particles

_____

In the liquid state, the particles

_____

In the gas state, the particles

_____

Hint: Do not confuse the particle movement and arrangement in different states. For help, see 5.1.2 States of matter.

⊗ **Pinchpoint review**

Now look back at the question – do you think you chose the right letter?
Turn to the Answers page to find out.

6.1.1 Chemical reactions

A Fill in the gaps to complete the sentences.

A chemical reaction is a change that makes _____ substances. In a chemical reaction, the atoms in

the starting substances are _____ and join together _____ . It is _____

easy to reverse a chemical reaction. Chemical reactions involve _____ transfers to or from the

surroundings. Not all changes involve chemical reactions. A _____ change, such as melting, is

usually reversible.

B The diagrams below show the atoms in some physical changes and chemical reactions.

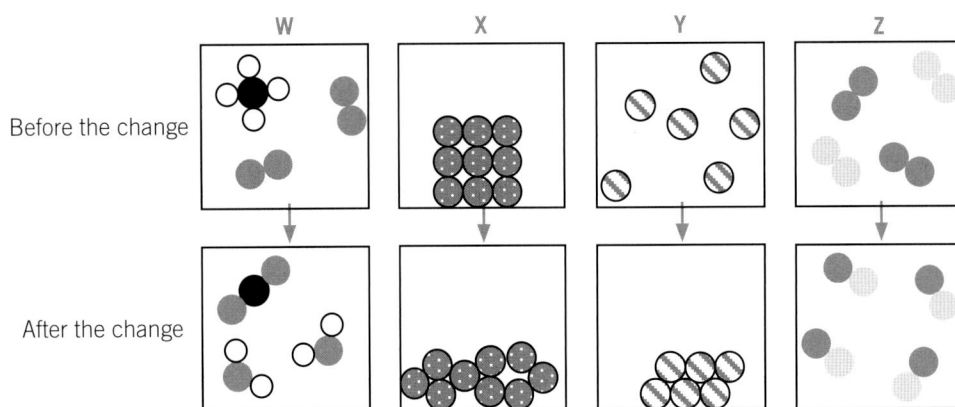

Before the change

After the change

W   X   Y   Z

a Write down the letters of the diagrams that show chemical reactions. _____

b Explain how you decided which diagrams show chemical reactions.

_____

C Tick to show whether each statement is true for chemical reactions, physical changes, or both.

Statement	✓ if true for chemical reactions	✓ if true for physical changes
In this type of change, new substances are made.		
This type of change is easily reversible.		
This type of change involves energy transfers.		
In this type of change, the atoms are rearranged and join together differently.		

D A student uses tongs to hold a piece of shiny magnesium metal in a Bunsen burner flame. He sees a bright white flame. Afterwards, all that is left is some white powder.

Decide whether the change is a physical change or a chemical reaction, and justify your answer.

_____

_____

E Write a paragraph to compare physical changes with chemical reactions.

_____

_____

_____

_____

6.1.2 Acids and alkalis

A Fill in the gaps to complete the sentences.

Do **not** taste or feel substances in science unless your teacher tells you to. Acids taste _____

and alkalis feel _____. Wear safety glasses or safety goggles when working with acids and alkalis

because some solutions of these substances are _____. This means that they burn eyes and

_____. Some solutions of acids and alkalis could make your skin red or itchy. This shows that they

are _____. A concentrated solution of alkali has more alkali particles in it than a _____

solution.

B This hazard symbol is displayed on bottles that contain some solutions of acids and alkalis.

Complete the table below.

Risk from this hazard	How to control this risk
damaging your eyes	
	wear plastic gloves

C Ms Khan has two bottles of sulfuric acid, **X** and **Y**. There is one litre of acid in each bottle.

- The acid in bottle **X** is concentrated.
- The acid in bottle **Y** is dilute.

a Predict one difference in the properties of the acids in bottles **X** and **Y**.

_____

b Give a reason for the difference you predicted in your answer to part **a**.
In your answer, compare the numbers of acid particles in the two bottles.

_____

c Suggest how Ms Khan could make the acid in bottle **X** more dilute.

_____

D All acidic solutions include a large number of the particles shown below on the left. All alkaline solutions include a large number of the particles shown below on the right.

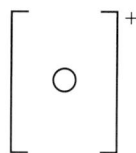

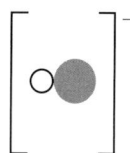

Key
○ hydrogen atom
● oxygen atom
+ the particle has a positive charge
− the particle has a negative charge

a Describe **one** way in which the particles in acids and alkalis are similar.

_____

_____

b Describe **two** ways in which the particles in acids and alkalis are different.

_____

_____

_____

6.1.3 Indicators and pH

A Fill in the gaps to complete the sentences.

Indicators show whether a solution is acidic, alkaline, or _____. Litmus indicator is red in acidic

solutions and _____ in alkaline solutions. Universal indicator is _____ or orange or

yellow in acids, green in _____ solutions, and blue or purple in _____ solutions. The

_____ scale measures how acidic or alkaline a solution is. The pH of an acid is _____

than 7. The pH of a _____ solution is 7. The pH of an alkali is _____ than 7.

B The table shows the colours of four indicators in dilute acids and alkalis.

Indicator	Colour in dilute hydrochloric acid	Colour in dilute sodium hydroxide solution (an alkali)
red cabbage	red	yellow or green
litmus	red	blue
methyl orange	red	yellow
phenolphthalein	colourless	pink

Ben adds a few drops of different indicators to some different solutions.
Draw a line to match each observation to a conclusion. You can choose an option more than once.

Observation

A colourless solution becomes yellow when a few drops of methyl orange are added.

A colourless solution remains colourless when a few drops of phenolphthalein are added.

A colourless solution becomes yellow when a few drops of red cabbage indicator are added.

Conclusion

The solution is neutral.

The solution is acidic.

The solution is alkaline.

C a Explain why there is uncertainty in pH values that are measured using universal indicator.

_____

b Describe a method of measuring pH that gives more accurate values than universal indicator.

_____

D The table gives the pH values of six solutions.

Solution	pH
U	7.1
V	3.2
W	9.5
X	13.8
Y	2.4
Z	3.7

a List the letters of the solutions in order of increasing acidity (most alkaline solution first).

_____

b Give the letters of three solutions that could be ethanoic acid.

_____

c Give the letter of the ethanoic acid solution that is most concentrated. _____
Explain your decision.

_____

6.1.4 Acid strength

A Fill in the gaps to complete the sentences.

In a solution of a strong acid, _____ of the acid particles split up. In a solution of a weak acid, only

_____ of the particles split up. Hydrochloric acid and sulfuric acid are _____ acids.

Ethanoic acid and citric acid are _____ acids. The concentration of a solution of an acid is the amount

of acid dissolved in water to make 1 _____ of solution.

B The table below shows the pH of 2 solutions of 4 different acids.
For each acid, draw a circle around the **more concentrated** solution.

Acid	pH of first solution of this acid	pH of second solution of this acid
hydrochloric acid	1	2
ethanoic acid	5	4
sulfuric acid	3	2
citric acid	4	5

C Each statement has one mistake in it. Use a coloured pen to correct the mistakes.

a In a solution of a strong acid, only some of the acid particles split up.

b In a solution of a weak acid, all the acid particles split up.

c A concentrated solution of ethanoic acid has less acid dissolved in it than a dilute solution of ethanoic acid.

d A concentrated solution of hydrochloric acid has a higher pH than a dilute solution of hydrochloric acid.

e The pH of a strong acid is higher than the pH of a weak acid, if the concentration of two acids is the same.

f The pH of an acid solution depends on acid strength only.

D Adam and Dan have a solution with a pH of 14.

a Suggest **two** safety precautions the students should take when using the alkali.

_____

b The students adds water to the solution, so its pH decreases to 9. Adam and Dan discuss what safety precautions to take with the more dilute solution.

Adam says, "The new solution is less hazardous. We can take fewer precautions now."

Dan says, "We must take the same precautions as before."

Name the student who is correct. Explain your decision.

Name: _____

Reason: _____

A Fill in the gaps to complete the sentences.

When a base reacts with an acid, the acid is _____ by the base. If you add a base to an acid, the pH _____. If you add an acid to a base, the pH _____.

B The soil on Frank's farm is acidic. He adds a base to the soil.

a Describe what happens to the pH of the soil when Frank adds the base.

_____

b Suggest why Frank wants to change the pH of the soil.

_____

_____

c Give one example of another useful neutralisation reaction.

_____

C Ash investigates three different types of indigestion tablets.
He measures the volume of acid that each tablet can neutralise.

Complete the table to show the different types of variable in Ash's investigation.

Type of variable	Variable
Independent	
Dependent	
Control	
Control	
Control	

D Samira adds an alkaline solution, 1 cm³ at a time, to an acid.

She uses a pH probe and data logger to measure the pH. The graph shows her results.

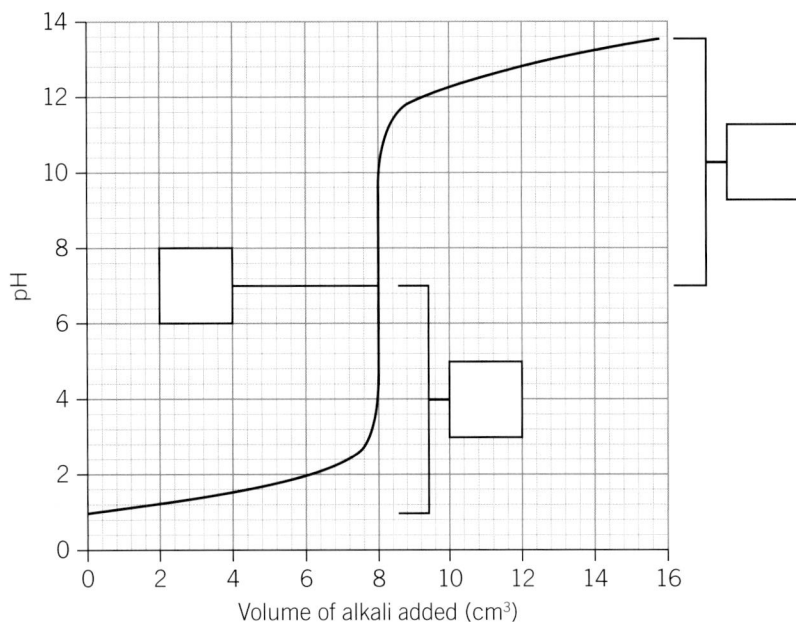

In each box, write the letters of **one or two** of the statements below.

V	The mixture is acidic.
W	All the acid has been neutralised.
X	The alkali is neutralising the acid.
Y	The mixture is neutral.
Z	The mixture is alkaline.

6.1.6 Making salts

A Fill in the gaps to complete the sentences.

When an acid reacts with a metal or a compound that includes a metal, one of the products is a

_____. Hydrochloric acid makes _____ salts. Sulfuric acid makes _____

salts. When an acid reacts to make a salt, metal atoms replace the _____ atoms that were in the acid.

B The statements below can be reordered to describe how to make a salt from zinc oxide and hydrochloric acid. Read the statements and write down the order of statements that you think will give the best description.

Best order ☐ ☐ ☐ ☐ ☐ ☐ ☐

1 Filter to remove unreacted zinc oxide.

2 Stop adding zinc oxide when some zinc oxide is left over.

3 Leave the evaporating dish and its contents in a warm, dry place.

4 Pour some dilute hydrochloric acid into a beaker.

5 Heat the zinc chloride solution in an evaporating basin.

6 Add zinc oxide powder to the acid, one spatula at a time, while stirring.

7 Stop heating when about half the water has evaporated.

C This apparatus is used to remove water from a solution of copper sulfate, which is a salt.

Label the diagram by writing the name of one substance, solution, or piece of apparatus on each answer line.

| evaporating basin | salt solution | beaker | boiling water |

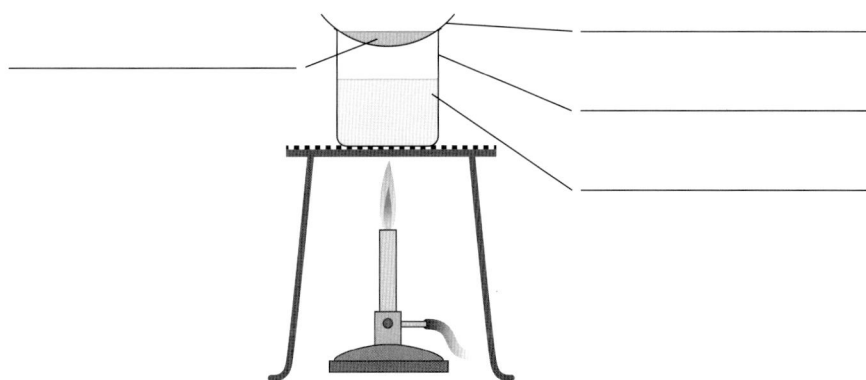

D Complete the table by adding the names of the salts formed in each reaction.

	Reactants	Name of salt formed	Name of other product formed
a	magnesium and sulfuric acid		hydrogen
b	zinc and hydrochloric acid		hydrogen
c	copper oxide and hydrochloric acid		water
d	sodium hydroxide and sulfuric acid		water
e	potassium hydroxide and hydrochloric acid		water

E There is a very vigorous reaction when a solution of acid **X** reacts with zinc. A solution of acid **Y** does not react with zinc.

a Predict which acid solution has the lower pH. _____

b Explain your answer to part **a**.

_____

_____

6.2.1 More about elements

A Fill in the gaps to complete the sentences.

An element is a substance that _____ be broken down into other substances, and that contains _____ type of atom. Elements in the Periodic Table are sorted into _____ and non-metals. Most _____ elements are shiny. They are good conductors of heat and _____. They also have _____ densities.

B Compare the properties of typical metal and non-metal elements. In your answer, write about **three** properties that are different for metals and non-metals.

_____

_____

_____

_____

_____

_____

C The table shows some properties of four elements: **Q**, **R**, **S**, and **T**. The letters given are **not** the chemical symbols of the elements.

Element	Appearance at 20 °C	Does it conduct electricity?	Density (g/cm³) at 20 °C	Melting point (°C)	Boiling point (°C)
Q	invisible	no	0.00018	−270	−269
R	brown	no	3.1	−7	59
S	silver and shiny	yes	14	−39	357
T	grey and shiny	yes	8.9	1453	2730

a Write down the letters of the two elements in the table that are probably non-metals.

_____ and _____

b Write down the letter of the one element in the table that is probably a metal, but that has one property that is not typical of metals. _____

Justify your choice.

_____

_____

c Write down the letters of two elements that are on the right of the stepped line in the Periodic Table.

_____ and _____

d Write down the letter of the element in the table that could be helium. _____

e Write down the letter of one element in the table that could be used to make electrical wires. _____

Justify your choice.

_____

f Write down the letter of one element in the table that could be used to fill balloons. _____

Justify your choice.

_____

6.2.2 Chemical reactions of metals and non-metals

A Fill in the gaps to complete the sentences.

Many elements react with oxygen to form _____. These reactions are called _____

reactions. Metal oxides and _____ oxides have different physical properties, for example, most

metal oxides are in the _____ state at room temperature, and most non-metal oxides are in the

_____ state. Metal oxides and non-metal oxides also have different chemical properties. For example,

many metal oxides are basic and many non-metal oxides are _____.

Word equations describe chemical reactions. In a word equation, the starting substances, called

_____, are on the left of the arrow. The substances that are made, called _____, are

on the _____ of the arrow. The arrow in a word equation means 'reacts to _____'.

B The diagram below shows some atoms in the reaction of hydrogen with oxygen to make water.
Label the diagram using the labels in the box.

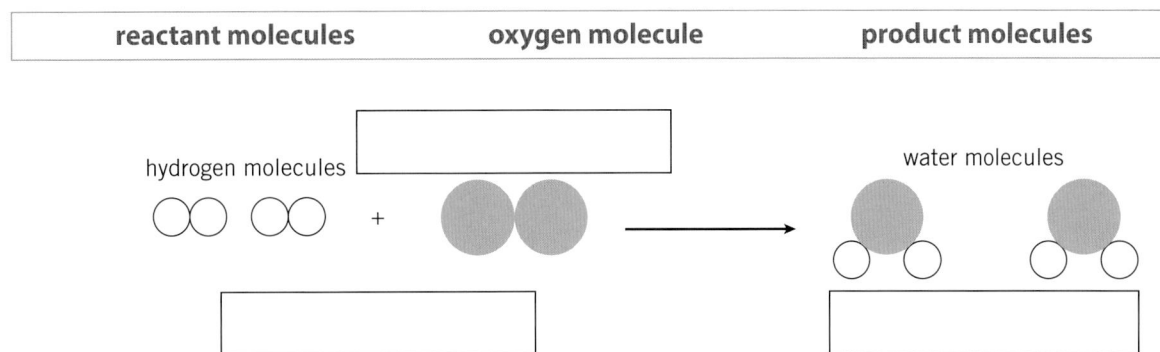

| **reactant molecules** | **oxygen molecule** | **product molecules** |

hydrogen molecules

water molecules

Hint: In a chemical reaction, the starting substances are called reactants. The substances that are made are called products.

C Write a word equation for each oxidation reaction below.

a Magnesium reacts with oxygen to make magnesium oxide.

_____

b Nitrogen reacts with oxygen to make nitrogen dioxide.

_____

c Potassium reacts with oxygen to make potassium peroxide.

_____

d Sulfur reacts with oxygen to make sulfur dioxide.

_____

D Look at the word equations you wrote to answer activity **C**.

Write down the names of **two** acidic oxides that are made in the reactions.

_____ and _____

6.2.3 Metals and acids

A Fill in the gaps to complete the sentences.

Around 80% of elements are _____. They have similar physical properties; for example, they are

shiny, and they conduct heat and _____. Metals also have patterns in their chemical properties. For

example, some metals react with dilute acids to make salts and _____ gas. Magnesium reacts with

dilute hydrochloric acid to make _____ chloride and hydrogen.

B **a** Complete the results table for the experiment.

Metal	Observations
magnesium	
zinc	
iron	

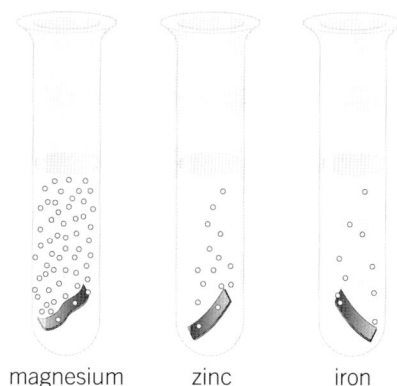

magnesium   zinc   iron

b Write a conclusion for Magda's experiment. In your conclusion, include the words in the box.

reactive	hydrogen	vigorous

_____

_____

C For each pair of reactants, predict the name of the salt formed.

a magnesium and hydrochloric acid   name of salt _____

b zinc and sulfuric acid   name of salt _____

c iron and hydrochloric acid   name of salt _____

D Write a word equation for the reaction that occurs between each pair of reactants in activity **C**.

Hint: Each pair of reactants reacts to make a salt and hydrogen.

a _____

b _____

c _____

E Junaid has three test tubes of hydrochloric acid. He measures the temperature in each test tube. Then he adds one piece of a different metal to each test tube. He measures the new temperature in each test tube. His results are in the table.

Metal	Temperature of acid before adding metal (°C)	Temperature of mixture after adding metal (°C)	Temperature change (°C)
iron	20	26	6
magnesium	21	36	
zinc	19	28	
copper	21	21	

a Complete the table by writing down the missing temperature changes.

b Write a conclusion to link the temperature changes in the table to the reactivity of the metals.

_____

_____

6.2.4 Metals and oxygen

A Fill in the gaps to complete the sentences.

Some metals react with oxygen from the _____. The more _____ the metal, the

more vigorous the reaction. For example, magnesium burns vigorously to make magnesium _____.

Copper does not burn when you heat it in a Bunsen burner flame. Instead, it forms a layer of black copper

_____ on its surface. Gold does not react with oxygen. It is an _____ metal.

The reactivity of an element is its tendency to take part in chemical _____. The greater the reactivity

of an element, the more _____ it reacts with other substances.

B Zion heats small pieces of five metals in a Bunsen burner flame.

She writes her observations in the table below

Metal	Observations when heated in a Bunsen burner flame
copper	Does not burn. Forms layer of black copper oxide on its surface
iron	Small pieces burn, but less vigorously than zinc
gold	No change in appearance
magnesium	Burns vigorously
zinc	Small pieces burn, but less vigorously than magnesium

Write a conclusion for Zion's experiment. In your conclusion, use the words in the box.

reactive	unreactive	vigorously	magnesium oxide	copper oxide

_____

_____

_____

_____

_____

C **a** Use the observations in the table in activity **B** to write the names of the
metals in order of reactivity, with the most reactive at the top.

_____

_____

b Explain the order of reactivity you chose in part **a**.

_____

_____

_____

_____

_____

D The table shows some properties of two metal elements: **X** and **Y**. The letters given
are not the chemical symbols of the elements.

Metal	How does the metal react with oxygen from the air at room temperature?	Does the metal conduct electricity?	Does the metal oxide conduct electricity?	Density (g/cm³) at 20°C
X	Quickly reacts to form a layer of the metal oxide on its surface	yes	no	0.97
Y	Does not react	yes	no	19

Which metal can be used to make electrical connectors? Justify your decision using information from the table.

Metal _____

Justification _____

6.2.5 Metals and water

A Fill in the gaps to complete the sentences.

The reactivity series lists the _____ in order of how vigorously they react. The metals at the _____ of the reactivity series react vigorously with water, oxygen, and dilute acids. The metals at the bottom of the reactivity series are _____. Metals that react with water include potassium, sodium, lithium, and calcium. The products of their reactions are _____ gas and the metal _____.

B Magnesium and potassium react with water. The diagrams show their reactions.

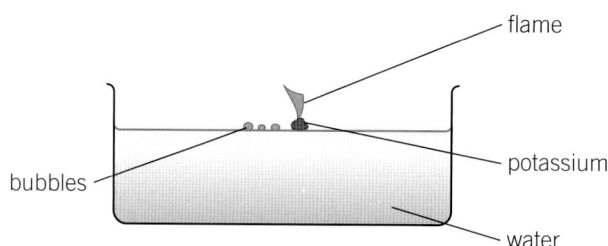

	Part of the reactivity series
	rubidium
	lithium
	calcium
	magnesium
	aluminium
	zinc
	iron
	lead
	copper
	silver
	gold

a Complete the table to compare the reactions of potassium and magnesium.

Metal	How vigorous is the reaction?	Name of the product that is formed in the gas state	Name of the other product
magnesium			
potassium			

b Write a paragraph, based on the information in the table, to compare the reactions of magnesium and potassium with water.

_____

_____

_____

_____

C Sarah has samples of three metals – calcium, magnesium, and silver. She does not know which metal is which.

a Describe a simple investigation Sarah could do to find out which metal is which. In your answer, name **two** variables that Sarah must control to make sure that the investigation is fair.

_____

_____

_____

b Explain how Sarah could use her results to decide which metal is which.

_____

_____

_____

Hint: Use the reactivity series on this page to help you.

6.2.6 Metal displacement reactions

A Fill in the gaps to complete the sentences.

Metals take part in displacement reactions. In a displacement reaction, a _____ reactive metal pushes out a _____ reactive metal from its compound. For example, in the thermite reaction, aluminium displaces iron from _____ _____. The products of the reaction are aluminium _____ and _____.

B The word equation shows a displacement reaction.

magnesium + copper sulfate solution ⟶ magnesium sulfate solution + copper

The statements below are about the reaction in the equation. There is one mistake in each statement. Use a coloured pen to correct each mistake.

a Magnesium is below copper in the reactivity series.

b Magnesium is less reactive than copper.

c Magnesium displaces copper from its compound, copper chloride.

d As the reaction takes place, the colour of the blue copper sulfate solution gets darker.

e As the reaction takes place, the piece of magnesium gets bigger.

C Draw a tick next to each pair of substances that you predict will react together.

Then use the reactivity series in C3.3 to explain your prediction for each of the three pairs of substances.

	Pair of substances	✔ if a reaction occurs	Scientific explanation of prediction
1	copper and magnesium chloride solution		
2	magnesium and lead oxide		
3	zinc and lead nitrate		

D The particle diagram below represents the displacement reaction of magnesium with copper oxide.

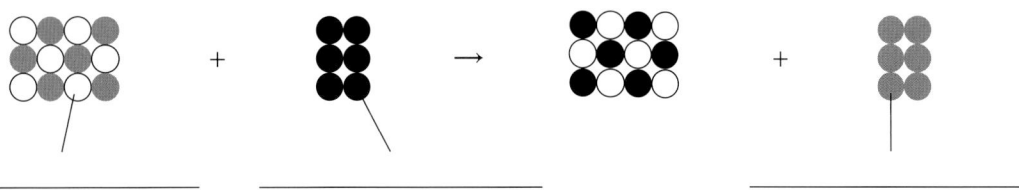

_____   _____   _____

a Label the diagram with the labels in the box.

| **magnesium atom**   **copper atom**   **oxygen atom** |

b Explain what the diagram shows.

_____

E Use ideas about the reactivity series to explain the observations below.

a Mike adds some small pieces of zinc to copper sulfate solution. A pink-brown solid forms, and the colour of the blue solution becomes paler.

_____

_____

b Bridie heats a mixture of iron and aluminium oxide powder. There is no reaction.

_____

_____

Pinchpoint question

Answer the question below, then do the follow-up activity **with the same letter** as the answer you picked.

Lyra has some acid. Its pH is 3. She adds water and measures the pH. Then she adds sodium hydroxide solution and measures the pH again.
Which set of results could be correct?

	pH at start	pH after adding water	pH after adding sodium hydroxide solution
A	3	8	1
B	3	2	1
C	3	4	5
D	3	2	5

Follow-up activities

A Each sentence below has one mistake. Write a corrected version of each sentence.

a Adding water to an acid makes the solution less dilute.

_____

b When an acid is diluted, it has more acid particles per litre.

_____

c The greater the number of acid particles per litre, the higher the pH.

_____

d Adding alkali to an acid dilutes some or all of the acid.

_____

e Neutralising an acid decreases the pH of the solution.

_____

f Adding water to an alkaline solution makes the solution less dilute.

_____

g Neutralising an alkali increases the pH of the solution.

_____

h The smaller the number of acid particles per litre, the lower the pH.

_____

i When an alkali is diluted, its pH increases.

_____

Hint: What happens to the pH as a solution gets less acidic? For help see 6.1.2 Acids and alkalis, 6.1.3 Indicators and pH, C6.1.4 Acid strength, and C6.1.5 Neutralisation.

B In each question below, circle the correct pH.

a   The most acidic solution   1   4   6

b   The most alkaline solution   8   11   14

c   The least acidic solution   2   3   5

d   The least alkaline solution   9   12   13

e   The neutral solution   6   7   8

f   The most acidic solution   1   5   7   9

g   The most alkaline solution   6   7   8   9

Hint: What is the pH range of acidic solutions? For help see 6.1.3 Indicators and pH.

C a Draw a line to match each action to the correct observation and explanation.

Action	Observation	Explanation
Adding water to an alkaline solution	pH increases, but not above 7.	Some of the alkali has been neutralised so there are fewer particles of alkali per litre.
Adding acid to an alkaline solution	pH increases, possibly above 7.	The solution has been diluted so there are fewer particles of acid per litre.
Adding water to an acidic solution	pH decreases, but not below 7.	Some of the acid has been neutralised so there are fewer particles of acid per litre.
Adding alkali to an acidic solution	pH decreases, possibly below 7.	The solution has been diluted so there are fewer particles of alkali per litre.

Hint: Can an acidic solution become alkaline when water alone is added to it? For help see 6.1.2 Acids and alkalis, 6.1.3 Indicators and pH, C6.1.4 Acid strength, and C6.1.5 Neutralisation.

b Adam has two solutions of hydrochloric acid, **X** and **Y**, as shown in the table.

Solution	Concentration (g/litre)
X	10
Y	20

Adam pours solution **X** into a beaker. He measures its pH. He then adds some solution **Y** to the same beaker, and measures the pH again.

i   Tick one box to predict whether the pH of the mixture of **X** and **Y** is:

• less than the pH of solution **X**   ☐

• the same as the pH of solution **X**   ☐

• more than the pH of solution **X**.   ☐

ii   Explain your prediction.

_____

_____

D The diagrams show two acid solutions.

One solution is more concentrated than the other.

Key

● Acid particle   ◯ Water particle

X

Y

Tick the statements below that are true.

1 Solution X has more acid particles per litre than solution Y. ☐

2 Solution X is less concentrated than solution Y. ☐

3 Solution Y is more dilute than solution X. ☐

4 Adding more water to solution X would concentrate the solution. ☐

5 Adding more water to solution Y would dilute the solution. ☐

Hint: Does a more concentrated acid have more or fewer acid particles per litre? For help see 6.1.2 Acids and alkalis.

Pinchpoint review

Now look back at the question – do you think you chose the right letter?
Turn to the Answers page to find out.

7.1.1 The structure of the Earth

A Fill in the gaps to complete the sentences.

The Earth is made up of four _____. In the centre is the solid _____ core, which

is surrounded by the liquid _____ core. Outside the outer core is the _____. This

is mainly _____ rock, but it can _____. On the surface of the Earth is the rocky

_____, which is between 8 km and 40 km thick. Most rocks are mixtures of naturally occurring

elements or compounds called _____.

B Write **three** sentences to compare the properties of the different layers of the Earth.

_____

_____

_____

C You can use a hard-boiled egg in its shell to model the structure of the Earth.

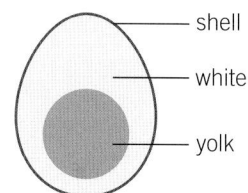

shell
white
yolk

a Give **two** ways in which the egg is similar to the structure of the Earth.

_____

_____

b Describe **two** ways in which the egg is not a good model for the structure of the Earth.

_____

_____

Hint: In your answer, write down how the model and the structure of the Earth are similar. Then write down how they are different.

D The table shows the percentage by mass of the five most common elements in the Earth's crust.

Element	Percentage by mass (to 2 significant figures)
oxygen	46
silicon	28
aluminium	8.3
iron	5.6
calcium	4.2

Scientists estimate that the mass of the Earth's crust is 24 trillion tonnes.

a Calculate the mass of silicon in the Earth's crust. Give your answer to two significant figures.

Mass of silicon = _____ trillion tonnes

b There is a mass of 1.3 trillion tonnes of element **X** in the Earth's crust.

Use data from the table to suggest the name of element **X**.

Element **X** is _____

7.1.2 Sedimentary rocks

A Fill in the gaps to complete the sentences.

There are three types of rock – igneous, sedimentary, and _____. Most types of sedimentary rock

are porous and _____ . Sedimentary rocks are formed when rock breaks up into smaller pieces by

physical, chemical, or _____ weathering. The smaller pieces, called _____, move

away from the rock and are carried far away by _____ processes. The sediments settle in one

place. This is _____. When layers of different types of sediment settle on top of each other, the

layers are called _____. Then the sediments in each layer join together by _____ or

_____. In _____, the weight of the sediments above _____ together

the sediments below. In _____, another substance sticks the sediments together.

B This question is about the formation of sedimentary rocks.

    a Name **three** types of weathering, and write down a definition for each type.

    _____

    _____

    _____

    _____

    _____

    _____

    b Explain what is meant by the phrase **transport of sediments**.

    _____

C Complete the table to explain each property of a typical sedimentary rock.

In your answers, refer to the structure of the rock, and how it was formed.

Property	Reason for property in terms of the structure of the rock and how it was formed
Porous	
Soft	

D Some students have a box of damp sand. They put a 1 kg weight on top of the sand.

The students are modelling one process in the formation of a sedimentary rock.

    a Name the process that the students are modelling.

    _____

    b Suggest one strength of the students' model.

    _____

    Hint: Write down how the model is like the process it represents.

    c Suggest one weakness of the students' model.

    _____

7.1.3 Igneous and metamorphic rocks

A Fill in the gaps to complete the sentences.

Underground, liquid rock is called _____. On the surface, liquid rock is called _____.

Igneous rocks form when liquid rock cools and _____. They are made up of _____, which are joined together with no gaps. This means that igneous rocks are _____-_____. They are also

durable and _____. Metamorphic rocks form when heat and/or high _____ change

existing rock. Metamorphic rocks are made up of _____, so they are non-porous.

B Salol is a compound that has a melting point of 42 °C. When hot liquid salol cools down in the lab, it freezes to make crystals. Maddie has some liquid salol. She places a few drops on a cold microscope slide, and a few drops on a warm microscope slide. She obtains the results shown opposite.

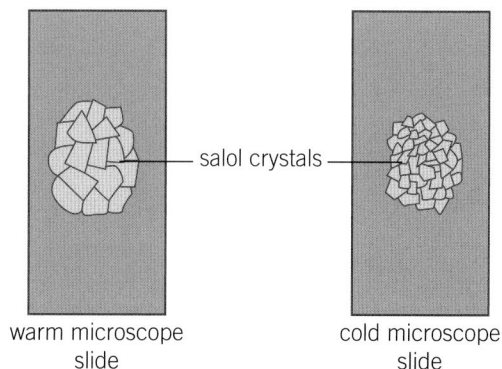

salol crystals

warm microscope slide

cold microscope slide

a Complete the table below to describe and explain the observations from Maddie's experiment.

Relative temperature of microscope slide	Observations	Explanation of observations
warm		
cold		

b Use information from the table you completed in part **a** to explain why igneous rock formed underground has bigger crystals than igneous rock formed on the surface.

_____

_____

_____

C Complete the table to explain each property of a typical igneous rock. In your answers, refer to the structure of the rock, and how it was formed.

Property	Reason for property in terms of the structure of the rock
Not porous	
Hard	

D A metamorphic rock has a fossilised shell in it. The shape of the shell is distorted.

a Explain whether the metamorphic rock was formed from a sedimentary rock or an igneous rock.

_____

_____

b Explain whether the metamorphic rock was formed by the action of heat or high pressure.

_____

_____

7.1.4 The rock cycle

A Fill in the gaps to complete the sentences.

The rock cycle shows how the materials in rocks are _____. For example, when a rock of any

type is weathered, its sediments may form _____ rocks. When a rock melts, the liquid rock later

cools and _____ to make _____ rock. When a rock experiences high pressures or

_____, its particles may be rearranged, forming _____ rock. When forces from

inside the Earth push rocks upwards, _____ occurs.

B Each number below represents a process that helps to convert rock from one type to another.

1	cooling	**6**	weathering
2	freezing	**7**	transport
3	melting	**8**	deposition
4	the action of heat	**9**	cementation
5	the action of high pressure	**10**	compaction

Label the diagram of the rock cycle by writing **one or more** numbers in each box. Use each number as many times as you need to.

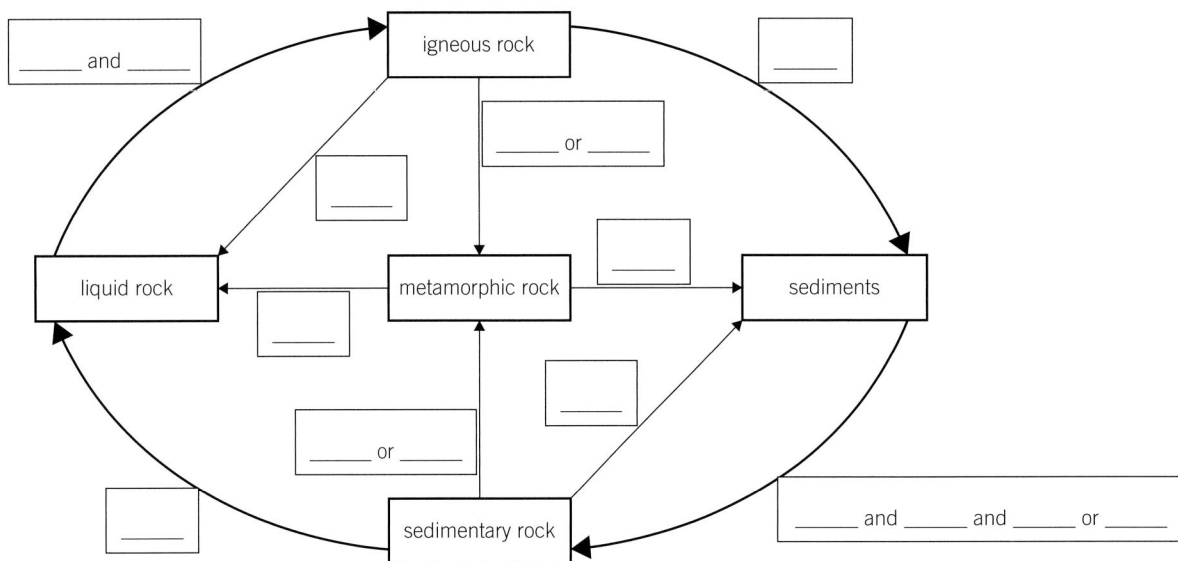

C Write a paragraph to describe one possible journey of some material around the rock cycle.

In your answer, include at least three steps.

For example, you might like to start with plant roots growing in a crack in the rock, and small pieces breaking off the rock. What might happen next?

There are many possible answers to this question.

_____

_____

_____

_____

_____

7.1.5 Ceramics

A Fill in the gaps to complete the sentences.

Ceramics are compounds. They include metal silicates, _____ oxides, and _____

carbides. Ceramics are hard, stiff, and brittle. They have very _____ melting points and are electrical

_____. These are _____ properties. Ceramics also have similar chemical properties to

each other – they do not react with water, acids, or _____.

B Draw **one** line to match each property to the statement that **best** explains why a ceramic material has this property.

Property	Best explanation of property

a Very hard

b Does not conduct electricity

c High melting point

1 Does not have charged particles that can move.

2 Needs a large amount of energy to break bonds between atoms.

3 The bonds between the particles are very strong.

C The table shows the properties of three materials, **X**, **Y**, and **Z**.

Material	Melting point (°C)	Does it conduct electricity?	Is it brittle?
X	3130	yes	no
Y	4215	no	yes
Z	from 120 to 180	no	no

a Write down the letter of one material in the table that could be a ceramic. _____

b Justify your choice in part **a**.

_____

Hint: Justify means that you have to use evidence from the information given in the table to support your answer.

D Ruby sets up the apparatus below to compare the strengths of different ceramic materials. She finds the mass that makes the piece of ceramic break.

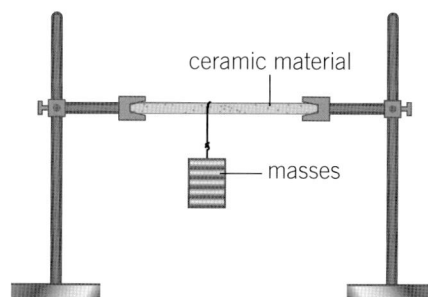
ceramic material
masses

Complete the sentences below.

a The independent variable is _____

b Two of the control variables are _____

c The purpose of the clamp, boss and clamp stand is _____

_____

d 100 g masses are used instead of 1 kg masses because _____

_____

e One measure to control risk in the investigation is _____

_____

A Fill in the gaps to complete the sentences.

We can see many different objects in the night sky without a telescope. The nearest are artificial satellites that

_____ the Earth. The Moon is the Earth's only _____ satellite. We can also see five

_____. Like Earth, they orbit the _____ and make up part of the _____

_____. The dots of light we see are _____ in our own _____, which

is called the _____ _____. It is just one of billions of galaxies that make up the

_____. Planets have been discovered that orbit _____ other than the Sun, called

_____. Astronomy involves distances so big that it is convenient to use a different unit, the distance

that light travels in one year, called a _____ _____.

B The Universe is so large that it affects how we observe distant objects.
Draw a line to match each object with the description of how it is observed.

Stars within our galaxy		cannot be seen without a telescope.
The most distant planets in our Solar System		appear as dots of light, even if we use a telescope.
Neighbouring galaxies		appear as a blur in the sky without a telescope – individual stars cannot be seen.

C Fill in the gaps to complete the sentences using the following keywords.

light years   **light minutes**   **light years**   **light second**

We use 'light time' to describe the distances to objects in the Universe. The Moon is one _____

_____ from Earth. The Sun is eight _____ _____ from Earth. Proxima

Centauri is the next nearest star after the Sun, at four _____ _____. Andromeda is the

nearest galaxy outside our own Milky Way, at two million _____ _____.

D Describe the structure of the Universe in detail, in order of size starting with the smallest objects.
Include the following keywords:

asteroids	**Milky Way**	**Universe**	**moons**	**Sun**	**planets**	**Solar System**

_____

_____

_____

_____

_____

7.2.2 The Solar System

A Fill in the gaps to complete the sentences.

There are _____ planets in the _____ _____ , which orbit the

_____ in an _____ orbit. We see the planets by _____ of the Sun's light.

The inner four planets, Mercury, _____ , Earth, and Mars, have a _____ composition

and the outer four, Jupiter, Saturn, _____ , and Neptune, have a _____ composition.

The inner ones are smaller and _____ , the outer ones larger and much _____ as they

are further from the Sun. Between the inner and outer planets there is an _____ belt made up of

thousands of pieces of rock. Pluto used to be called a planet but is now called a _____ planet.

B **a** Various objects are visible in the sky.

Tick which ones emit their own light, and which ones can be seen because they reflect light from another source.

Object	✓ if emits own light	✓ if reflects light from another source
Sun		
Planets		
Moons		

b Fill in the gaps to complete the paragraph below about the lights we see in the night sky.

Planets do not _____ light, but we see them in the sky because they _____ light

from the _____ . They appear to move back and forth across the sky because they are moving in

_____ around the _____ .

C Look at the data in the table for the first seven planets in the Solar System.

Planet	Diameter (km)	Distance from Sun (millions of km)	Temperature (°C)	Composition	Number of moons	Has rings
Mercury	4800	58	−180 to 430	Rocky	0	No
Venus	12 000	110	470	Rocky	0	No
Earth	13 000	150	−89 to 58	Rocky	1	No
Mars	6800	230	−82 to 0	Rocky	2	No
Jupiter	140 000	780	−150	Gas giant	67	Yes
Saturn	120 000	1400	−170	Gas giant	62	Yes
Uranus	51 000	2900	−200	Gas giant	27	Yes

a Explain how the properties and features of planets are linked to their place in the Solar System.

_____

_____

_____

_____

b An eighth planet, Neptune, was discovered beyond Uranus, orbiting at 4500 million km from the Sun.

Use the data in the table to predict the features and properties of Neptune.

_____

_____

A Fill in the gaps to complete the sentences.

Once each _____, the Earth _____ on its axis, causing the Sun's apparent motion

through the sky and giving us day and _____. Once each _____, the Earth

_____ around the Sun. The differences between summer and winter in the UK are mainly caused

by the _____ of the Earth's axis. In summer, the Northern Hemisphere tilts _____ the

Sun, which means that each bit of the ground receives _____ of the Sun's rays. The groups of stars,

or _____, that we see in the summer at night are _____ from the stars that we see in

the winter. This is because the Earth is moving around the _____. The side of the Earth that has night

is facing different stars at different times of the _____.

B Draw a line to match the object with the description and explanation of the apparent movement of the object in the sky.

the Moon		the Earth orbits the Sun once a year and the night-side of the Earth faces different constellations of stars during the year
the Sun		the Earth spins on its axis once every 24 hours and so different regions of the Earth face the Sun at different times of day
stars		orbits the Earth once a month

C Consider the data in the table below.

City, country	Latitude (degrees north of equator)	Daylight hours on 'longest' day (hours)
Accra, Ghana	5	
Rabat, Morocco	34	14.4
Plymouth, UK	50	16.4
Aberdeen, UK	57	17.9
Iqaluit, Canada	63	

a Predict how the average temperatures in these cities compare during summer in the northern hemisphere. Give a reason for your answer.

_____

_____

_____

_____

b Use the data above to predict the number of daylight hours in Accra and Iqaluit on the longest day.

Accra: _____ hours   Iqaluit: _____ hours

D Suggest how seasons in a country such as the UK would be different if the Earth's axis of rotation was not tilted.

_____

_____

_____

7.2.4 The Moon and changing ideas

A Fill in the gaps to complete the sentences.

One side of the Moon is lit by the _____ at all times. As it orbits the _____ we see

different amounts of it illuminated by the Sun, causing the _____ of the Moon. An outdated model

of the Solar System says that the Earth does not move; it is called the _____ model. New evidence

led to the development of the _____ model we use today.

B Look at the diagram of the Moon orbiting the Earth.

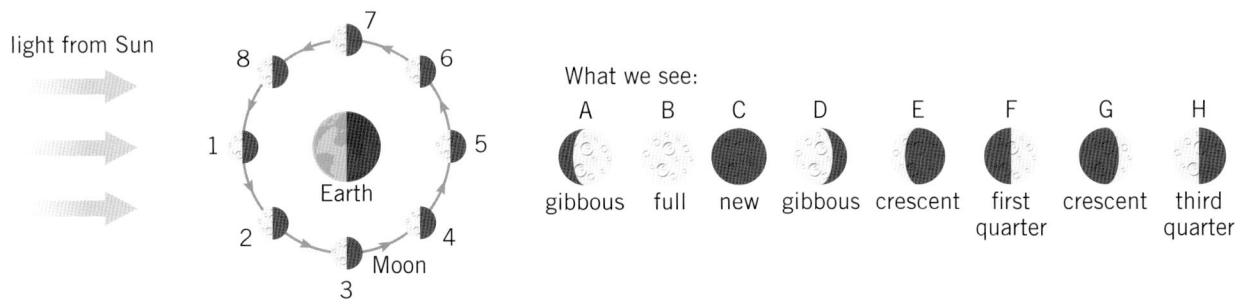

light from Sun

What we see:

A	B	C	D	E	F	G	H
gibbous	full	new	gibbous	crescent	first quarter	crescent	third quarter

For each position 1–8 on the diagram, write down a letter A–H in the table below, to show which phase of the Moon is seen by someone on Earth.

Position	1	2	3	4	5	6	7	8
Phase of the Moon (A–H)								

C Imagine that a particular lunar month has 28 days, so that on day 1 there is a new moon.
Predict which phase occurs for each of the following days.

Day of lunar month	Phase of the moon
8	
15	
22	
26	
29	

D The table shows four pieces of evidence relating to geocentric and heliocentric models of the Solar System.

a Tick the one that was seen as supporting the older geocentric model.

b Tick the two that were found by Galileo using the newly discovered telescope, and that support the heliocentric model.

	Evidence	✓ if supported the older geocentric model	✓ if discovered using the telescope
1	Sometimes some planets appear to move backwards through the sky		
2	The Earth does not seem to move underneath our feet		
3	Some moons appear to orbit Jupiter		
4	The planet Venus has phases like the Moon		

E a Lunar eclipses occur when the Earth blocks the Sun's light from reaching the Moon. They all occur in one phase of the Moon. Suggest which phase this is.

_____

b Solar eclipses occur when the Moon blocks the Sun's light from reaching the Earth. They all occur in one phase of the Moon. Suggest which phase this is.

_____

Hint: Think about where the Sun, Moon, and Earth must be to cast each shadow. See 4.2.1 Light for help.

Pinchpoint question

Answer the question below, then do the follow-up activity **with the same letter** as the answer you picked.

Astronomers have been able to work out where objects are in the Universe.

Which of these statements is true?

A The Sun orbits the Earth in our Solar System.

B Our Solar System is made up of a star with planets that orbit it.

C The order of scale (smallest to largest) is Earth, Sun, Milky Way, Solar System, Universe.

D The Milky Way is a galaxy in our Solar System.

Follow-up activities

A The Earth orbits the Sun.

Name three different types of object which orbit our Sun.

_____

_____

Hint: Which objects are in our Solar System? For help see 7.2.1 The night sky.

B Choose which option correctly indicates the distances from the Earth of: the Moon, the Sun, Proxima Centauri (nearest star beyond the Sun), and Andromeda (nearest galaxy beyond the Milky Way).

Distance from ...	Option 1	Option 2	Option 3
... Moon to Earth	500 000× Earth diameter	4× Earth diameter	30× Earth diameter
... Sun to Earth	300 000× further away than the Moon	20× further away than the Moon	400× further away than Moon
... Proxima Centauri to Earth	400× further away than the Sun	5000× further away than the Sun	300 000× further away than Sun
... Andromeda to Earth	30× further away than Proxima Centauri	200× further away than Proxima Centauri	500 000× further away than Proxima Centauri

Hint: What are the light-distances to other objects? For help see 7.2.1 The night sky.

C The Milky Way is our galaxy and consists of billions of stars. Our Solar System consists of the planets orbiting one of those stars – the Sun.

Draw a diagram to show the structure of our Solar System, and which objects orbit which others. Include the following: the Moon, the Earth, Jupiter, and the Sun.

Hint: What do planets orbit? For help see 7.2.1 The night sky.

D The Milky Way is our galaxy and consists of billions of stars. Our Solar System consists of the planets orbiting one of those stars – the Sun.

a Write the order for the objects in the table below, with '1' being the nearest to the Earth.

b Tick each object that is within the Milky Way.

Object	Order (1 is nearest Earth)	✓ if within Milky Way
Proxima Centauri (next nearest star beyond Sun)		
Sun		
Jupiter		
Moon		
Andromeda galaxy		

Hint: Where are the nearest stars? For help see 7.2.1 The night sky.

Pinchpoint review
Now look back at the question – do you think you chose the right letter?
Turn to the Answers page to find out.

Section 2 Revision questions

1 ⚗⚗ Fingerprints help to solve crimes, but fingerprints on plastic are often invisible. Forensic scientists can use gold to make fingerprints visible. They place a tiny amount of solid gold in a container with the piece of plastic. They take the air out of the container, and make the gold sublime. A thin film of solid gold deposits on the plastic, and the fingerprints become visible.

   a Gold is an element. Define the term 'element'.

(1 mark)

_____

   b Give the chemical symbol of gold. *(1 mark)*

_____

   c Use the particle model to explain subliming.

(2 marks)

_____

_____

_____

   d Explain why subliming is a physical change, not a chemical reaction. *(2 marks)*

_____

_____

_____

_____

2 ⚗⚗ A student has 95 g of water. He adds sugar to the water and makes a solution. The mass of the solution is 102 g.

   a Name the solute in the solution. *(1 mark)*

_____

   b Calculate the mass of sugar added to the water. *(2 marks)*

_____ g

3 ⚗⚗ Sam works at a swimming pool. The pH of the water should be 7.4. Sam checks the water pH every day. **Table 1** shows some of his results.

Table 1

Day	pH
Monday	7.8
Tuesday	7.4
Wednesday	7.0
Thursday	6.9

   a On which day is the water in the pool acidic?

(1 mark)

_____

   b Give the type of substance that Sam should add to the pool on Monday. Explain your answer.

(2 marks)

_____

_____

   c The substance that Sam adds to the pool has the hazard label shown in **Figure 1** on it.

Suggest one safety precaution that Sam should take when using this substance. *(1 mark)*

Figure 1

_____

4 ⚗⚗ Doctors give zinc sulfate tablets to people with big skin burns. A student makes zinc sulfate crystals from zinc oxide and an acid. This is the method used.

Step 1 Add zinc oxide to dilute acid. Stop adding when some zinc oxide is left over.

Step 2 Filter the mixture.

Step 3 Pour the zinc sulfate solution into an evaporating dish.

Step 4 Heat until all the water has evaporated.

   a Name the acid the student needs in step 1.

(1 mark)

_____

   b Write a word equation for the reaction in step 1. *(1 mark)*

_____

   c Name the substance left in the filter paper in step 2. *(1 mark)*

_____

d Suggest one improvement to step 4 to make the crystals as big as possible. *(1 mark)*

_____

e Write down two safety precautions the student should take in step 4. *(2 marks)*

_____

_____

5 ⚗⚗ Some students investigate indigestion tablets. They measure the volume of acid that each tablet can neutralise. Their results are in **Table 2**.

Table 2

Type of tablet	Volume of acid that the tablet can neutralise (cm³)			
	first measure-ment	second measure-ment	third measure-ment	mean
X	10	9	10	
Y	2	2	2	
Z	5	11	5	

a Name the type of substance that must be present in all three tablets, in order to neutralise the acid. *(1 mark)*

_____

b Circle the outlier in **Table 2**. *(1 mark)*

c Calculate the mean volume of acid needed to neutralise tablet **X**. Show your working. *(2 marks)*

_____

d The students decide to plot their results on a line graph. Explain why it is better to draw a bar chart, not a line graph. *(1 mark)*

_____

_____

e Write a conclusion for the investigation. *(1 mark)*

_____

_____

6 ⚗⚗ A teacher has samples of three metals: potassium, calcium, and magnesium.

a Describe an experiment the teacher could do to compare the reactivity of the three metals.

In your answer, identify **two** control variables and explain how the observations will show which metal is most reactive. *(4 marks)*

_____

_____

_____

_____

_____

_____

b Suggest **one** safety precaution the teacher should take in the experiment you described in part **a**, other than wearing eye protection. *(1 mark)*

_____

7 ⚗⚗ Here is part of the reactivity series, in decreasing order of reactivity.

magnesium
zinc
iron
lead
copper
silver

Which **two** pairs of substances take part in displacement reactions? Tick **two** boxes. *(2 marks)*

copper and silver nitrate solution ☐
iron and zinc nitrate solution ☐
lead and iron chloride solution ☐
magnesium and copper chloride solution ☐

8 ⚗⚗ Many types of sedimentary rock are porous.

a Explain what porous means. *(1 mark)*

_____

b Explain why a sedimentary rock is porous. *(1 mark)*

_____

_____

9 ⚗⚗ In the rock cycle, the materials that make up rocks are recycled. Describe how the conversions below may occur.

a Sedimentary rock to igneous rock. (Involves two stages) *(2 marks)*

_____

_____

b Igneous rock to sedimentary rock. (Involves four stages) (*4 marks*)

_____

_____

_____

_____

10 🧪🧪 **Figure 2** shows the positions of the Moon and some of the stars in the constellations Capricorn and Sagittarius in the night sky.

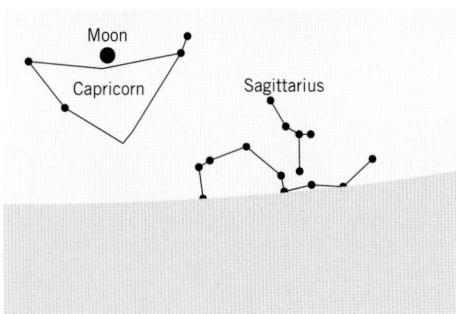

Figure 2 Day 1, 00:00

Figure 3 shows the same view of the night sky, one hour later.

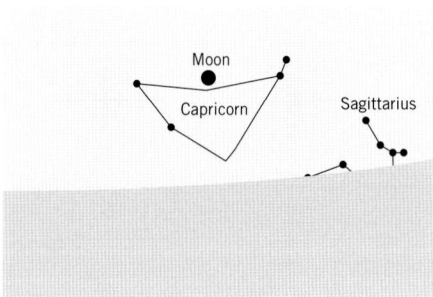

Figure 3 Day 1, 01:00

Figure 4 shows the same view of the night sky the next night at the same time as **Figure 1**.

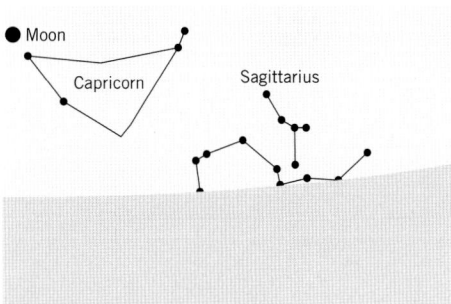

Figure 4 Day 2, 00:00

Explain why the positions of the Moon and stars are different in **Figures 3** and **4** compared to **Figure 2**. (*4 marks*)

_____

_____

_____

_____

11 🧪🧪🧪 Describe the differences and similarities between evaporating and boiling. Use the particle model to explain the differences. (*6 marks*)

_____

_____

_____

_____

_____

_____

_____

_____

_____

12 🧪🧪🧪 Draw a line to match each particle diagram to its description. (*3 marks*)

Particle diagram   **Description**

a mixture of two compounds

a pure element

a mixture of two elements

a mixture of an element and a compound

13 🧪🧪🧪 **Table 3** shows some properties and uses of three elements.

Table 3

Element	Melting point (°C)	Boiling point (°C)	State at 20 °C	Appearance	Other properties	Uses
mercury	−39	357		Shiny and silver-coloured	Does not react with substances in the air	Tilt switches, which set off an alarm if someone shakes a vending machine
platinum	1769	4530		Shiny and silver-coloured	Does not react with substances in the air	Jewellery, catalytic converters in cars, hard disks in computers
silver	961	2210		Shiny and silver-coloured	Reacts with hydrogen sulfide in polluted air to make black silver sulfide	Jewellery and ornaments

a Complete the table by writing down the state of each element at room temperature, 20 °C.   (*1 mark*)

b Compare the properties of mercury, platinum, and silver.   (*3 marks*)

_____

_____

_____

_____

_____

_____

_____

_____

c Using the information given in the table, explain why silver and platinum are used to make jewellery.   (*1 mark*)

_____

d Suggest one advantage of using platinum to make jewellery, compared to silver.   (*1 mark*)

_____

_____

_____

_____

e A tilt switch sets off an alarm when a vending machine is shaken, or turns off an electric heater if it falls over.

Identify the one property that is different for mercury and platinum that makes mercury suitable for making tilt switches while platinum is unsuitable.   (*1 mark*)

_____

_____

_____

14 🧪🧪🧪 Calculate the distance travelled by light in a light-year. Give your answer in metres. The speed of light is 300 000 000 m/s. A year has 365 days.   (*2 marks*)

_____

15 🧪🧪🧪 In a lunar month of 29 days, the new moon always occurs on day 1. Predict on which day

a the first quarter moon will occur   (*1 mark*)

_____

b the first full moon will occur.   (*1 mark*)

_____

16 🧪🧪🧪 **Table 4** shows data for two exoplanets, with two planets for comparison. These exoplanets both orbit stars that have similar masses to the Sun. Suggest values for the missing properties for each of the exoplanets and complete the table.   (*4 marks*)

Table 4

Planet	Average distance from star it orbits (Earth = 1)	Mass (Earth = 1)	Type of planet
Earth	1.0	1	Rocky
Jupiter	5.2	318	Gas giant
Exoplanet A	0.04		
Exoplanet B	3.6		

Section 2 Checklist

Revision question number	Outcome	Topic reference	🙁	😐	🙂
1	Explain sublimation based on the arrangement and movement of particles.	5.1.5			
2	Use data to draw a conclusion about the mass of solute dissolved in a solution.	5.2.2			
3a	Use the pH scale to measure acidity and alkalinity.	6.1.3			
3b	Explain how neutralisation reactions are used in a given situation.	6.1.5			
3c	Identify and describe the meanings of hazard symbols and offer suitable safety precautions.	EP2			
4a, b, c, d	Describe the steps in making a salt in a neutralisation reaction.	6.1.6			
4e	Suggest suitable safety precautions in an experiment.	EP2			
5	Design an investigation to find out which indigestion remedy is 'better'.	6.1.5			
6a	Plan a practical to compare the reactivity of three metals, including identifying control variables and planning how to control them.	6.2.5			
6b	Suggest suitable safety precautions in an experiment.	EP2			
7	Predict if a given pair of substances will react in displacement reactions.	6.2.6			
8	Explain why a sedimentary rock has a particular property based on how it was formed.	7.1.2			
9	Use the rock cycle to explain how the material in rocks is recycled.	7.1.4			
10	Explain the motion of the Sun, stars, and Moon across the sky.	7.2.3			
11	Compare evaporation, boiling, and sublimation based on the arrangement, movement, and energy transfers of particles.	5.1.5			
12	Use particle models to compare mixtures and pure substances.	5.2.1			
13	Justify the use of specific metals and non-metals for different applications, using data provided.	6.2.1			
14	Use the speed of light to describe distances between astronomical objects.	7.2.1			
15	Predict phases of the Moon at a given time.	7.2.4			
16	Make deductions from observation data of planets, stars, and galaxies.	7.2.2			

8.1.1 Levels of organisation

A Fill in the gaps to complete the sentences.

_____ organisms have five levels of organisation. This is called a _____. Cells are the building blocks of life. Groups of similar cells working together are called _____ and different tissues working together are called an _____. A group of different organs that work together is called an _____ _____. Finally, an _____ is made up of a number of organ systems working together to perform all the processes needed to stay alive.

B Describe what is meant by each of the following key terms:

a Tissue _____

b Organ _____

c Organ system _____

C Organise the following into a hierarchy, starting with the smallest, and list the level of organisation it belongs to.

dog	circulatory system	blood	heart	red blood cell

Structure   **Level of organisation**

_____   _____

_____   _____

_____   _____

_____   _____

_____   _____

D Other than blood, name a type of a tissue found in the heart and describe its function.

_____

_____

E Explain why multi-cellular organisms need organ systems to keep their cells alive.

_____

_____

_____

A Fill in the gaps to complete the sentences.

Your _____ is made up of bones. The skeleton has four functions: to _____ your organs,

to _____ the body, to help you _____, and to make red and white _____

cells. These cells are made in bone _____, which is found in the centre of some bones. Your muscles

and skeleton together make up the _____ _____ system.

B Together all the bones in your body make up your skeleton.

Label the missing bones on the diagram.

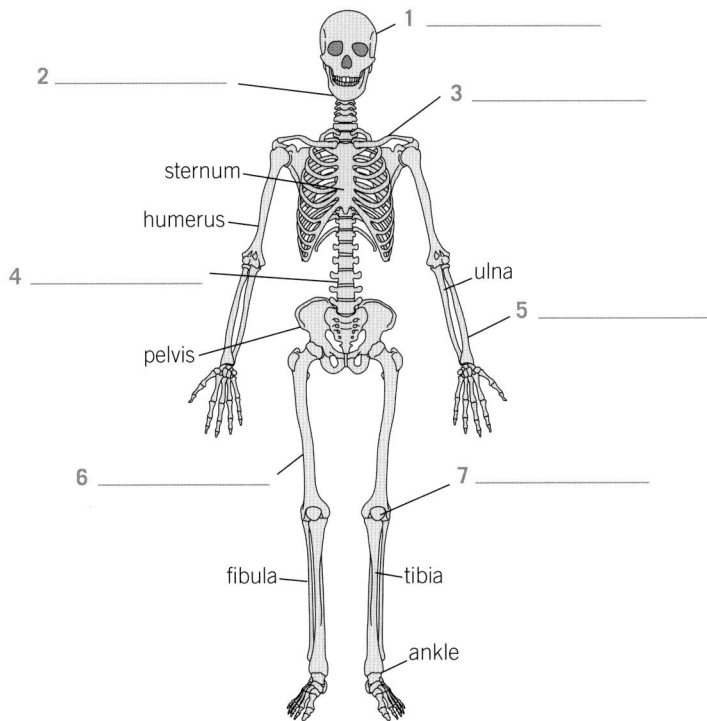

1 _____

2 _____

3 _____

sternum

humerus

4 _____

ulna

5 _____

pelvis

6 _____

7 _____

fibula   tibia

ankle

C Describe how the skeleton enables you to move. Include the terms **muscles** and **joints** in your answer.

_____

_____

_____

_____

D Describe **three** functions of the skeleton, other than movement.

1 _____

2 _____

3 _____

E Give an example of a bone and the organ it protects.

Bone _____   Organ _____

A Fill in the gaps to complete the sentences.

_____ are where bones join together. Different types of joint allow _____

in different _____. Bones are held together in a joint by _____. The

ends of bones in a joint are covered with _____ to stop them rubbing together. When

a muscle _____ it exerts a _____ on a bone, which is measured in

_____ (N), and it pulls the muscle in a certain direction. This is called biomechanics.

B Different joints allow movement in different directions.

  a Describe the difference in movement in the knee and shoulder joints. Use the terms **ball and socket** and **hinge**.

    _____

    _____

  b Explain why the joints in the skull are unusual.

    _____

    _____

C You can carry out simple experiments to measure the force of different body muscles. Explain how you could measure the force of your triceps muscle (the muscle in the back of your arm).

  _____

  _____

  _____

D a Label the parts of the knee joint in the diagram below.

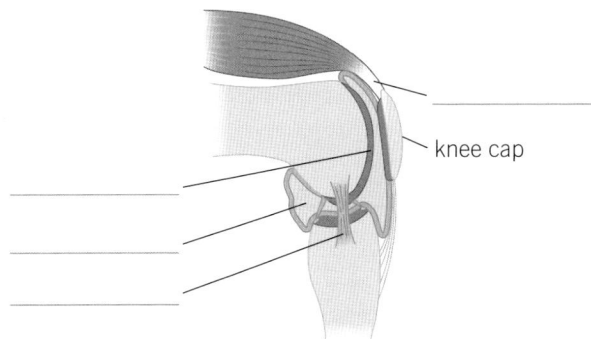

    knee cap

  b Describe the function of the following parts of the knee joint.

    Tendon _____

    Ligament _____

    Cartilage _____

    Fluid _____

  c Name the part of the bone that produces blood cells. _____

8.1.4 Movement: muscles

A Fill in the gaps to complete the sentences.

Muscles are attached to bones by _____. When a muscle contracts it _____ and

pulls on a _____. Pairs of _____ work together at a _____ to cause

movement. These are called _____ muscle pairs. As one muscle in the pair contracts the other

muscle _____.

B Muscles have a range of functions in the body.

Describe the main function of the muscles in the:

a heart _____

b intestine _____

c leg _____

C Describe what is meant by the term 'antagonistic muscle pairs'.

_____

_____

_____

D The diagram shows a leg and four of the major muscles involved in movement: A, B, C, and D.

With reference to the muscle pairs labelled A–D, explain how:

a the knee bends.

_____

_____

b toes point upwards.

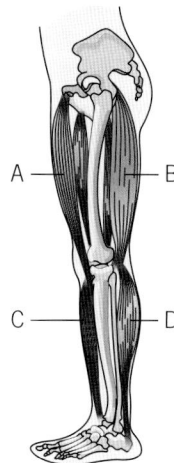

_____

_____

E Describe what is meant by the term 'muscle fatigue'.

_____

_____

8.2.1 Observing cells

A Fill in the gaps below to complete the sentences.

All living organisms are made up of _____ – these are the building blocks of life. To see cells in detail

you need to use a _____. This _____ the object. Looking carefully and in detail at an

object is called making an _____.

B A light microscope is used to magnify objects.

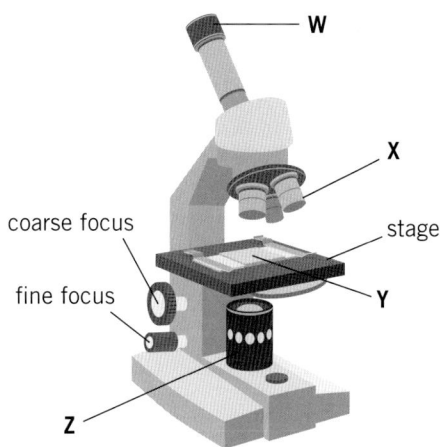

Match each missing label on the diagram to the correct word below.
Write **W**, **X**, **Y**, or **Z** beside each word.

slide ☐   eyepiece lens ☐

objective lens ☐   light ☐

C Henry wants to observe a leaf under the microscope. He takes a small piece of leaf and places it on a microscope slide. He places the slide on the stage of the microscope.

a Describe what he should do next to observe the leaf.

_____

_____

_____

b Explain how Henry could observe the leaf in greater detail.

_____

c Henry observed the leaf using an eye piece lens of ×10 magnification and an objective lens of ×50 magnification.

Calculate the total magnification he used.

_____

8.2.2 Plant and animal cells

A Fill in the gaps below to complete the sentences.

Plant and animal cells both contain a _____ that controls the cell, _____ where

chemical reactions take place, a _____ _____ that controls what comes in and out

of the cell and _____ where respiration occurs. Plant cells also contain a rigid _____

_____ that provides support, _____ for photosynthesis, and a _____

that contains cell sap to keep the cell firm.

B Label the main components in the animal and plant cells below.

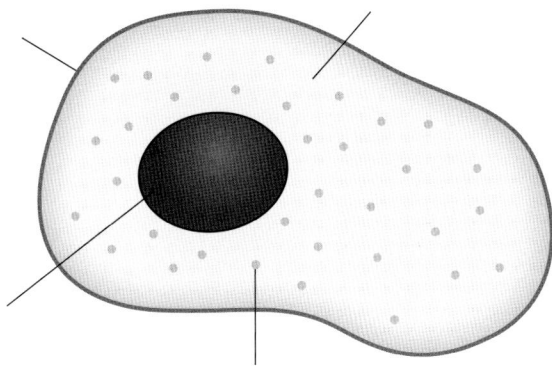

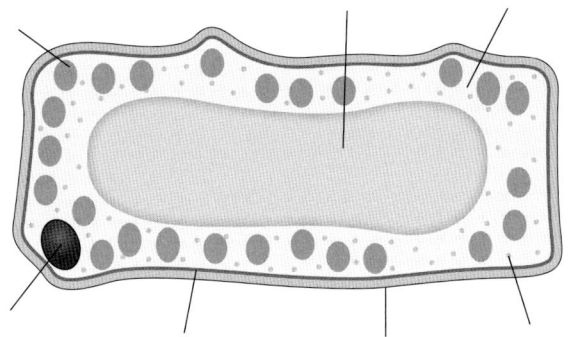

C List four components found in **both** animal and plant cells, and describe their functions:

Component   **Function**

1 _____   _____

2 _____   _____

3 _____   _____

4 _____   _____

D Explain the function of the following plant cell components.

a Chloroplasts

_____

b Vacuole

_____

c Cell wall

_____

E Name the fibre that makes up plant cell walls.

_____

8.2.3 Specialised cells

A Fill in the gaps to complete the sentences.

Some cells have special structural adaptations to carry out their functions. These cells are called

_____ cells. For example, in animals, _____ _____ cells have

haemoglobin for carrying oxygen, and nerve cells are long and thin to carry electrical _____.

_____ cells have a head and tail so they can carry male genetic material to the female egg. In plants,

root _____ cells have a large surface area to absorb _____ and nutrients from the soil

and leaf cells are packed with _____ to carry out photosynthesis.

B Name each type of specialised cell described below:

    a   Contains genetic information from the female parent _____

    b   Transmits electrical impulses around your body _____

    c   Packed with chloroplasts to maximise photosynthesis _____

C Circle **true** or **false** for the following statements about red blood cells.

For incorrect statements, correct the sentence so that it is true.

    a   They carry oxygen around the body.   **true / false**

    b   They have a nucleus.   **true / false**

    c   They have a disc-like shape.   **true / false**

    d   They contain chlorophyll.   **true / false**

D This is a sperm cell.

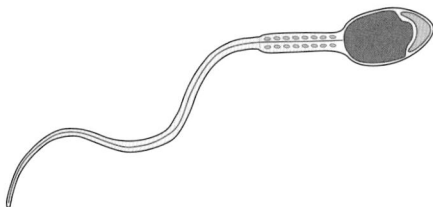

Explain why it has the following features.

    a   Tail: _____

    b   Lots of mitochondria: _____

    c   Streamlined head: _____

E Identify this specialised cell and explain how it is adapted to its function.

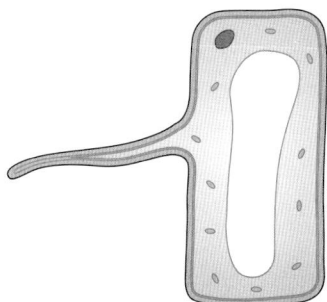

_____

_____

8.2.4 Movement of substances

A Fill in the gaps to complete the sentences.

Substances move from an area where they are in a _____ concentration to an area where they are

in a _____ concentration. This process is called _____. Many substances move into

and out of your cells by using this process. For example, in gas exchange, _____ diffuses into your

cells from the blood and _____ diffuses out of your cells into the blood, so that it can be taken to the

lungs and breathed out.

B Many substances move into and out of your cells by diffusion.

List **two** substances that diffuse **into** your cells from the blood.

1 _____   2 _____

C Two different liquids were placed in a container (**A**).

Complete the diagram to show how the molecules have moved after 10 seconds (**B**), and after 2 minutes, (**C**), as a result of diffusion.

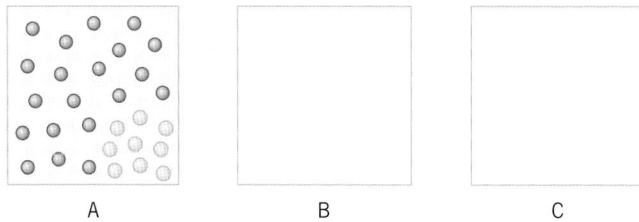

| A | B | C |

D Explain how water moves into a plant from the soil.

_____

_____

_____

E If a plant is not watered regularly it will wilt.

Explain how watering the plant will enable the plant to stand upright.

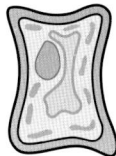

cell from a leaf   cell from a leaf
with no water   with enough water

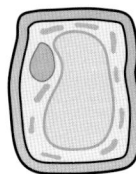

Hint: Use the information in the diagram to help you.

_____

_____

_____

_____

8.2.5 Uni-cellular organisms

A Fill in the gaps to complete the sentences.

Amoebas and _____ are examples of _____ organisms. This means that they consist

of only _____ cell. Both organisms have a cell membrane filled with _____ and

contain a nucleus. Euglenas also have _____, which make them look green, an _____

_____ which detects light, and a _____ so they can 'swim'.

B Uni-cellular organisms reproduce by binary fission to produce two identical cells.

Describe the **two** main steps in this process.

Step 1 _____

Step 2 _____

C This is a euglena. It lives in fresh water.

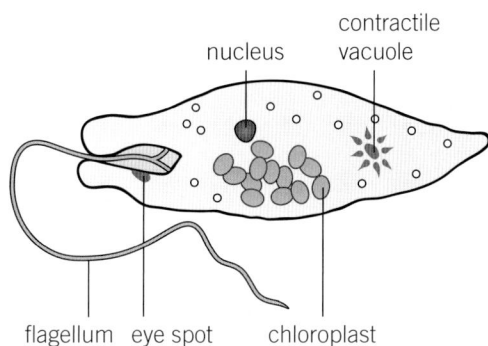

Give the function of the:

a Flagellum _____

b Chloroplasts _____

c Eye spot _____

D Euglenas have chloroplasts but they are not plants. Explain why.

_____

_____

E Amoebas cannot photosynthesise. Explain how they take in food.

_____

_____

_____

Pinchpoint question

Answer the question below, then do the follow-up activity **with the same letter** as the answer you picked.

Which of the following best describes the process of diffusion?

A The movement of particles from an area of high concentration to an area of low concentration.

B The process plants use to suck water into their roots.

C The random movement of particles from low to high concentration.

D The process by which water molecules move into a cell.

Follow-up activities

A The data in the table show how the surface area affects how quickly diffusion can take place:

Surface area (cm²)	10	20	30	40	50
Diffusion rate (arbitrary units)	2	4	6	8	10

a Describe any patterns shown in the data.

_____

_____

b Suggest the diffusion rate of a cell which has a surface area of 25 cm². _____

c Explain why many body cells are adapted to have a large surface area.

_____

_____

_____

_____

Hint: Think about what your body needs to survive. For further help see 8.2.4 Movement of substances.

B Look at the diagram and explain what is happening.

Use the following words in your explanation:

because	diffuse	concentration

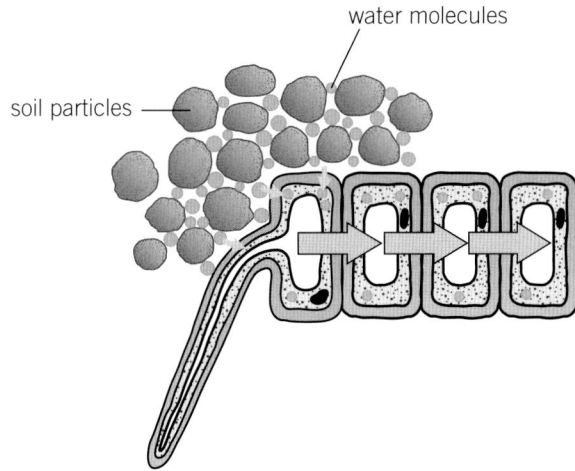

water molecules

soil particles

_____

_____

_____

_____

_____

Hint: Start your answer by explaining why water molecules move into the first cell. For further help see 8.2.4 Movement of substances.

C This diagram shows how you smell burnt toast in another room.

a In each row, if there is a difference in concentration, circle the box with the highest concentration of 'burnt-toast smell' particles.

Kitchen	Hallway	Living room
toast burns		
after 1 minute		
after 5 minutes		

• grey dots = air particles   • black dots = 'burnt-toast smell' particles

Hint: Highest concentration = area where there are the most particles. For further help see 8.2.4 Movement of substances.

b Now complete the following sentences.

The particles that make up the smell of burnt toast move from a place of _____ concentration

to a place of _____ concentration. Diffusion continues until there is the _____

concentration of 'burnt-toast smell' particles everywhere.

D The plant cell in the first diagram was placed into salt water that had a very low concentration of water.

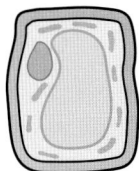

After a few minutes the cell looked like the second diagram.

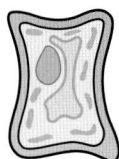

a Add an arrow to the first picture to show the direction of the movement of water molecules.

b Write a sentence explaining why water moves into or out of the cell.

_____

_____

_____

Hint: Where was the highest concentration of water molecules at the start of the experiment? For further help see 8.2.4 Movement of substances.

Pinchpoint review

Now look back at the question – do you think you chose the right letter?
Turn to the Answers page to find out.

9.1.1 Food chains and webs

A Fill in the gaps to complete the sentences.

A _____ _____ is a diagram that shows the transfer of _____ between organisms.

The first organism is always a _____. It transfers energy from the Sun into glucose by _____.

The other organisms in the chain are _____. They eat other organisms to gain energy. An animal that is

eaten by another organism is called a _____ organism. The animal that eats it is called a _____.

Most animals have more than one food source. This can be shown on a _____ _____. These

diagrams show a set of _____ food chains. _____ are organisms also found in food webs. They

recycle nutrients back into the _____ or water.

B Describe the difference between a food chain and a food web.

_____

_____

_____

C This food web shows the relationships between organisms in a garden.

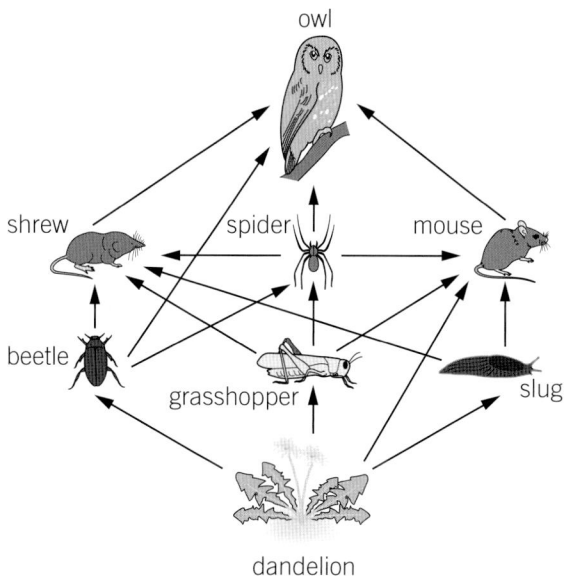

a Using information from the food web, draw a food chain with four links.

_____ ⟶ _____ ⟶ _____ ⟶ _____

b On your food chain, label which organism is each of the following:

producer	carnivore	herbivore	predator	prey

D Explain why many food chains have no more than four links.

_____

_____

_____

105

9.1.2 Disruption to food chains and webs

A Fill in the gaps to complete the sentences.

Living organisms depend on other organisms to survive. This is called _____. The number of organisms of a particular species in an area is called a _____. If the size of one population increases, it can change the size of another population. For example, if a producer population increases, the consumer population may _____.

Toxic chemicals can build up in the organisms in a food chain. This is called _____.

B Look at this food chain found in the sea: plankton ⟶ small fish ⟶ shark

Mercury is found at low levels in the sea, which is taken in by plankton. Mercury is toxic to humans.

Pregnant women are advised not to eat shark meat due to the high levels of mercury sometimes found in sharks; however, this advice does not apply to eating smaller fish that live in the same area. Explain why.

_____

_____

_____

_____

C This graph shows what happens to the population of native ocean fish when lionfish (a new predator) was introduced to an area.

Explain the trends shown in the population sizes in the graph.

_____

_____

_____

_____

_____

_____

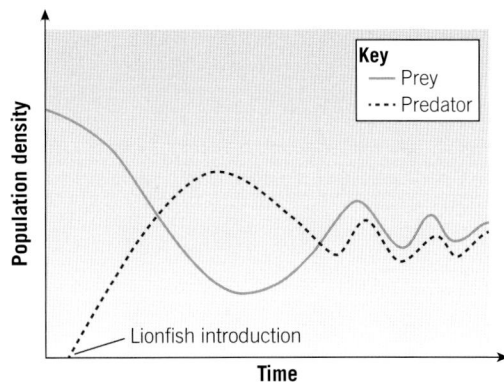

D Wolves have recently been reintroduced into Yellowstone National Park in the USA. Use the information below to explain how the interdependence of organisms has caused changes to rivers within the national park.

- Elks feed on willow trees.

- Elks are eaten by wolves.

- Beavers eat willow and use the branches to make dams.

_____

_____

_____

_____

9.1.3 Ecosystems

A Fill in the gaps to complete the sentences.

The place where an organism lives is called a _____. The organisms living in a particular area are called a

_____. The organisms and the area where they live is known as an _____. Different organisms

living together in the same place at the same time are said to _____. This is possible because they have

their own _____ – a particular place or role within the ecosystem.

B A group of students looked at the organisms present in an oak tree ecosystem. They found birds, ants, squirrels, woodlice, and slugs living on the oak trees.

    a Complete the sentences below to describe differences in the organisms' niches.

        Birds and squirrels both live in the tree canopy. They can co-exist as they have different _____

        _____ .

        Squirrels and woodlice can co-exist as they are found in different _____.

    b In the sentences above, circle the habitat and underline the community.

C A scientist investigated the distribution of plants at different distances from a hedgerow. Using the equipment below, they took measurements every 5 metres from the hedgerow.

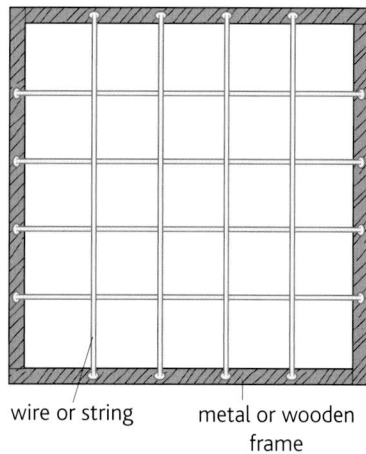

wire or string   metal or wooden frame

    a **i** Name the piece of equipment the scientist used. _____

        ii Name the type of habitat the scientist is investigating. _____

    b Suggest one reason for the change in distribution that the scientist observes.

    _____

    c Explain why the measurements are unbiased.

    _____

    _____

9.1.4 Competition

A Fill in the gaps to complete the sentences.

In order to survive, plants and animals compete for _____ such as water and space. Animals also compete for _____ to reproduce, and for _____. Plants compete for water and for _____ for photosynthesis and _____ for healthy growth. When a predator has only one main food source, there is an _____ between the predator and prey populations. A change in the population of one directly causes a change in the other. For example, if the prey population increases, the predator population _____ as they have more _____, meaning more stay alive to reproduce.

B Give **three** resources that plants compete for and what the plants need these for.

1 _____

2 _____

3 _____

C Animals also compete for resources.

a Name **one** resource other than food and water that an animal species competes for.

_____

b Describe why it needs this resource.

_____

c A new species of animal is introduced to the area, which competes for food.

Suggest and explain what could happen to the original animal population.

_____

_____

D A population of rabbits lives in a field. Foxes are predators of rabbits.

Study the graph opposite.

a Label the lines to show which represents the population of foxes and which represents the population of rabbits.

b Tick the boxes next to all the correct statements.

W As the number of rabbits goes up, the number of foxes goes down. ☐

X When the number of rabbits goes down, the amount of grass in the field decreases. ☐

Y As fox numbers increase, the population of rabbits decreases. ☐

Z As the number of rabbits increases, so does the number of foxes. ☐

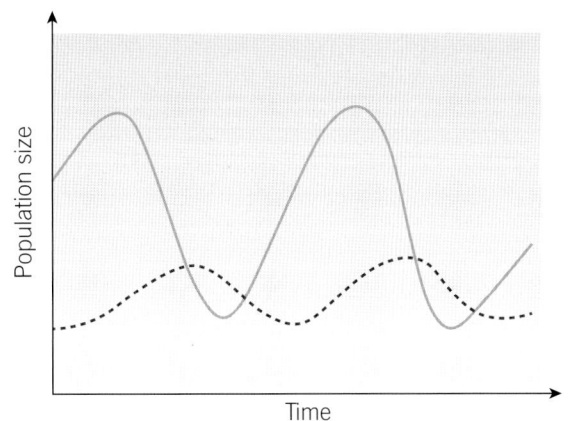

c Explain the trends you have identified.

_____

_____

9.2.1 Flowers and pollination

A Fill in the gaps to complete the sentences.

Pollination is the name given to the transfer of _____ from the _____ to the stigma. Pollen can be carried by the wind or by _____. To attract insects, flowers are often _____ coloured, contain _____ and are _____ smelling. Wind-pollinated plants produce _____ amounts of _____ pollen. Their anthers and _____ hang outside the flower.

B Complete the labels of the flower structures on the diagram.

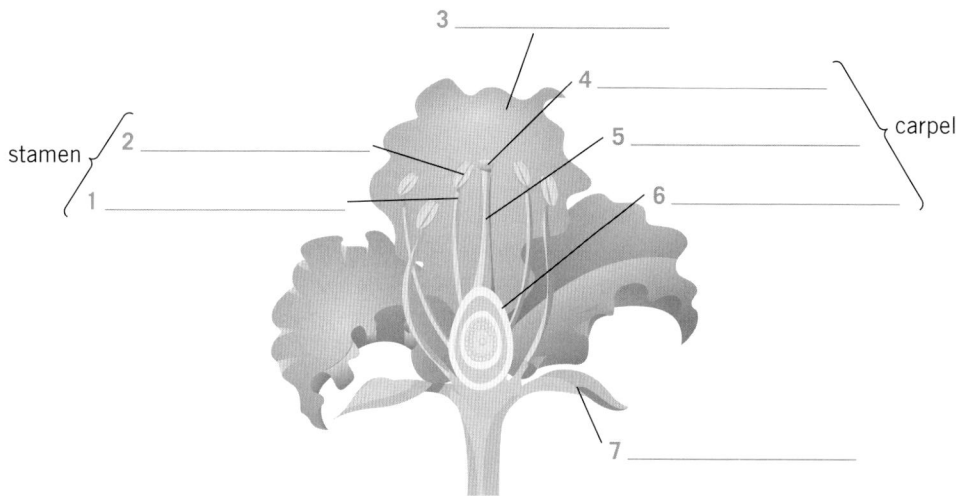

3 _____

4 _____

stamen
2 _____
1 _____

5 _____

6 _____

carpel

7 _____

C Describe the process of pollination.

_____

_____

D Tulips are pollinated by insects. Explain **three** ways the flower is adapted for this type of pollination.

1 _____

2 _____

3 _____

E Explain the differences in the types of pollen produced by insect-pollinated and wind-pollinated plants.

_____

_____

_____

A Fill in the gaps to complete the sentences.

During _____, the nucleus of the _____ grain and the _____ join

together. The ovary then develops into the _____ and the ovules become _____.

To grow a new plant, the seed needs to _____. For this to occur it needs _____,

water, and oxygen.

B Label the diagram below, showing the main structures involved in fertilisation.

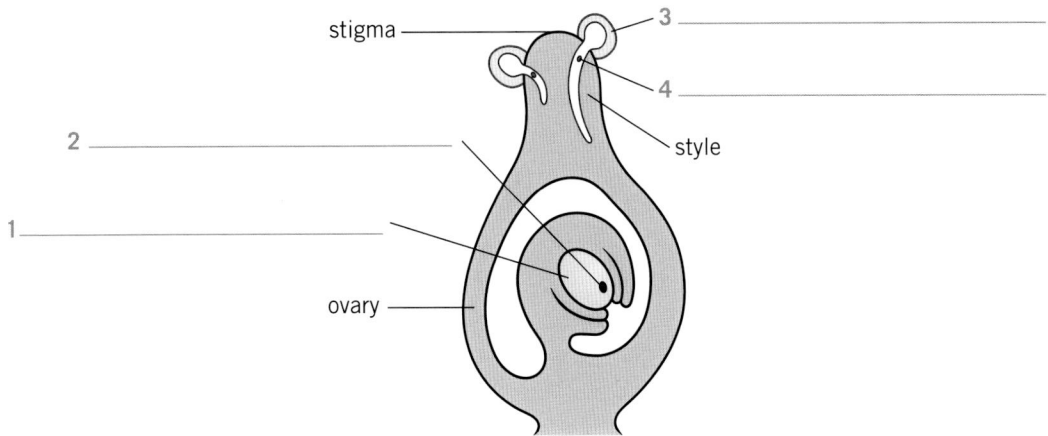

C Describe the processes that occur after pollination, including fertilisation and seed formation.

_____

_____

_____

_____

D Complete the flow diagram to explain the main steps in germination. Use the key words:

shoot	seed coat	root	light

1 Seed absorbs water rapidly – _____
↓

2 _____
↓

3 _____
↓

4 First leaf appears – _____

Hint: For help with this activity, look back at the germination diagram in 9.2.2 of the Student Book.

E A student planted 25 seeds, but only 18 of the seeds germinated.

Calculate the percentage of seeds that germinated.

_____ %

9.2.3 Seed dispersal

A Fill in the gaps to complete the sentences.

Seeds are _____ away from the parent plant to reduce _____. This increases their

chances of survival as they have more _____ and nutrients to grow. Seeds can be dispersed by the

_____, explosion, _____, and water.

B Name the method of seed dispersal used by the following seeds and describe how the seed is adapted to its method of dispersal.

a

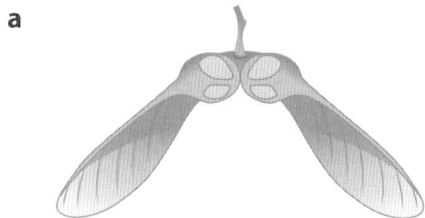

Method _____

Adaptation _____

_____

_____

_____

b

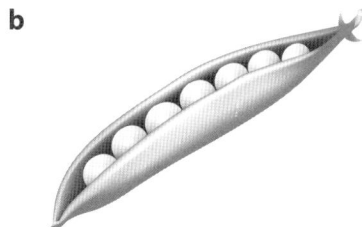

Method _____

Adaptation _____

_____

_____

_____

C Explain why seeds are dispersed.

_____

_____

D A group of students carried out an investigation to see if seeds with larger wings travel further when blown by a fan.

   a Write a suitable hypothesis for this investigation.

_____

_____

_____

   b Identify the types of variable used in their investigation. Include the units of measurement in your answers.

      i independent variable _____

      ii dependent variable _____

      iii control variable _____

Big Idea 9 Pinchpoint ⊗

Pinchpoint question

Answer the question below, then do the follow-up activity **with the same letter** as the answer you picked.

Which of the following statements best describes fertilisation in plants?

A Fusion of nuclei of male and female gametes.

B Movement of seeds away from the parent plant.

C Transfer of pollen from anther to stigma.

D When male and female cells meet.

Follow-up activities

A Look at the diagram of a flower.

Explain how this plant is adapted to increase the chances of pollination and describe the process of seed formation. Include the word **fertilisation** in your answer.

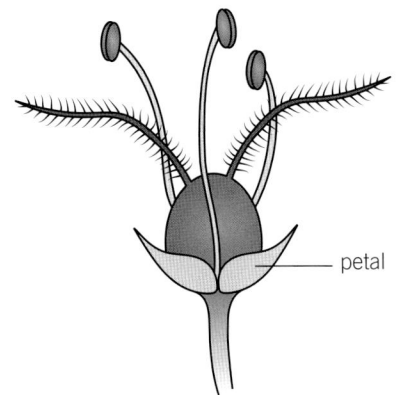
petal

_____

_____

_____

_____

Hint: Is this a wind-pollinated or insect-pollinated plant? For further help see 9.2.1 Flowers and pollination.

B Complete the following sentences on fertilisation and seed dispersal using key words from the box.

| pollen | dispersal | ovule | wind | style | seeds | nucleus | fruit | fertilisation |

Most plants grow from _____. To make a seed, male and female sex cells need to join together.

_____ (the male sex cell) is transferred to the stigma by the _____, or through being carried by

animals. It then grows a pollen tube down the _____ until it reaches an _____ (female sex cell)

in the ovary. The _____ of the pollen grain travels down the tube and fuses with the nucleus of the ovule.

This is called _____.

The ovary develops into the _____ and the ovules become seeds. To give the seed the best chance of

survival, they need to be spread far away from each other and their parent. This is called seed _____.

Hint: Dispersal means spreading out. For further help see 9.2.2 Fertilisation and germination.

C In order to make a seed, both pollination and fertilisation need to occur. Read the statements and write down the order you think will give the best description.

Correct order ☐ ☐ ☐ ☐ ☐ ☐

1 Pollen nucleus travels down tube.

2 This is called fertilisation.

3 Pollen nucleus fuses with ovule nuclei.

4 This is called pollination.

5 Pollen from the anther is transferred to the stigma.

6 The pollen grain grows a tube down the style and into an ovule in the ovary.

Hint: Pollination has to occur first and is helped by insects or wind. For further help see 9.2.2 Fertilisation and germination.

D Add a caption under each picture to describe the steps that take place to allow fertilisation to occur.

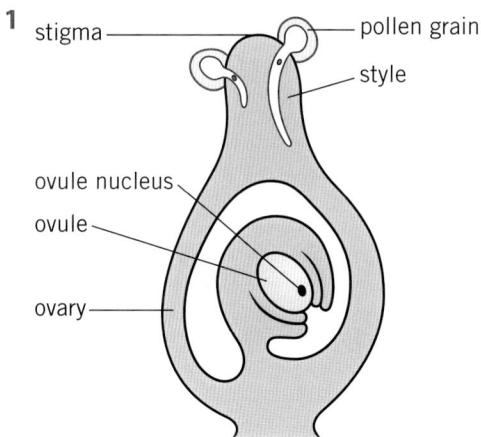

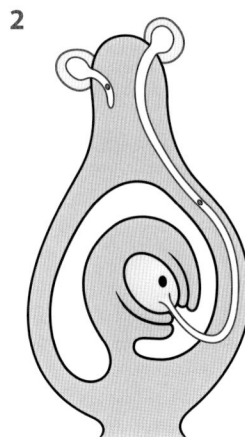

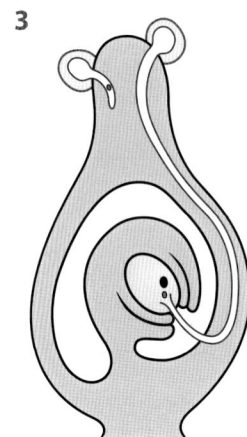

1 stigma —— pollen grain

style

ovule nucleus

ovule

ovary

2

3

_____ _____ _____

_____ _____ _____

_____ _____ _____

_____ _____ _____

Hint: Use the terms pollen tube, pollen nucleus, ovule nucleus. For further help see 9.2.2 Fertilisation and germination.

⊗ Pinchpoint review

Now look back at the question – do you think you chose the right letter?
Turn to the Answers page to find out.

10.1.1 Variation

A Fill in the gaps to complete the sentences.

Organisms from the same _____ can reproduce to produce fertile offspring. Differences in their

characteristics are known as _____. This can be caused by _____ variation –

characteristics that have been passed on from their parents such as eye colour. It can also be caused by an

organism's surroundings – _____ variation; for example, the amount of light a plant receives.

However, many characteristics are affected by both causes.

B Variation between individuals may be due to inherited variation, environmental variation, or both.

Draw a line to match each human variation to its cause.

Variation

| eye colour |

| height |

| accent |

| pierced ears |

| blood group |

| skin colour |

Cause

| inherited |

| environment |

| a combination of both |

C Describe the difference between environmental and inherited variation.

_____

_____

_____

D A cat had eight kittens.

   a Explain why the kittens did not all look identical.

_____

_____

_____

   b Explain why the differences in the kittens' appearance became greater as they got older.

_____

_____

_____

10.1.2 Continuous and discontinuous

A Fill in the gaps to complete the sentences.

Characteristics that can only result in certain categories or values show _____ variation; for example, gender. This type of variation should be plotted on a _____ _____ . Characteristics that can result in any value within a range show _____ variation; for example, height. This type of variation should be plotted on a _____ .

B Sort the following characteristics into those which show continuous variation and those which show discontinuous variation.

| leg length | blood group | leaf surface area | flower colour | fish mass | number of spots |

Continuous variation	Discontinuous variation

C Describe what is meant by a characteristic that shows:

a Continuous variation

_____

b Discontinuous variation

_____

D A group of students investigated the height tomato plants grow to over a six-week period.

a **i** What type of variation is plant height? _____

  ii What is the cause of the variation in plant height?

_____

_____

_____

b Name the type of graph they should use to display their measurements.

_____

10.1.3 Adapting to change

A Fill in the gaps to complete the sentences.

To help them survive, plants and animals have special characteristics called _____ Plants and animals have

to cope with changes in their _____. For example, in winter, trees lose their _____ and sheep

grow thicker _____. Sudden changes such as fire or disease mean that only the best _____

organisms survive and reproduce.

B Look at the diagram of a cactus.

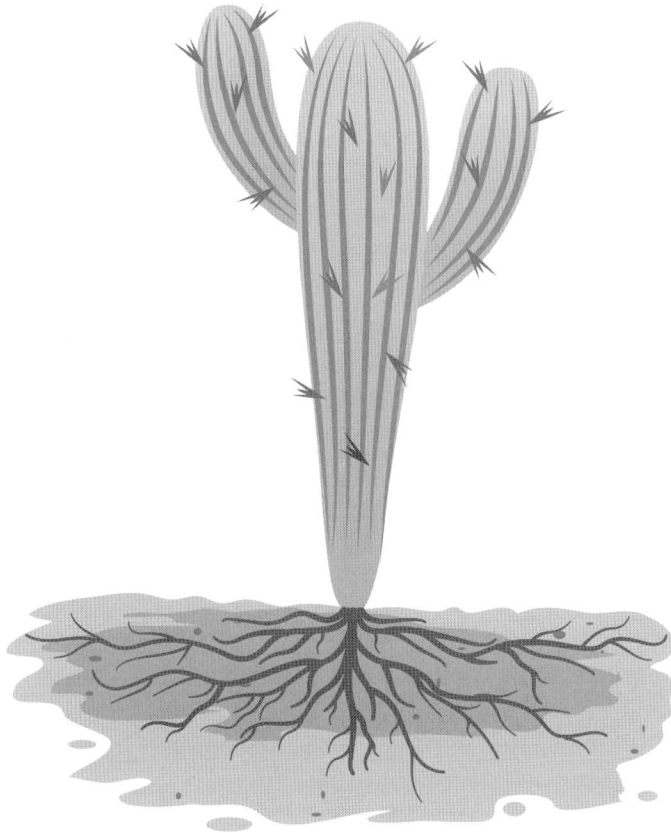

Label **three** adaptations on the cactus and explain how each adaptation helps the cactus to survive in a desert.

C Explain **one** way a plant and **one** way an animal copes with the seasons changing from summer to winter.

Plant _____

_____

Animal _____

_____

D Explain how competition for a food source can lead to changes in the population of that species.

_____

_____

_____

10.2.1 Adolescence

A Fill in the gaps to complete the sentences.

The period of time when a person develops from a child into an adult is known as _____.

The _____ changes that take place are called _____. These changes are

caused by _____ _____. Both males and females grow _____

and get _____ hair. Boys' voices _____ and their _____ widen.

Girls will start their _____ and their _____ widen.

B Describe the difference between adolescence and puberty.

_____

_____

_____

C Girls and boys undergo a number of **physical** changes during puberty.

Describe the main changes that occur – in boys, girls, or both – using the table below.

Boys	Girls

D Explain why the following changes take place during puberty.

a Girls' hips widen.

_____

_____

b Girls develop breasts.

_____

_____

10.2.2 Reproductive system

A Fill in the gaps to complete the sentences.

The function of the male reproductive system is to make _____ cells and release them

inside a female's _____. Sperm are made in the _____, which are contained

in the scrotum. They then pass through the _____ _____ and urethra, and

are then released from the _____ during sexual intercourse. The function of the female

reproductive system is to release _____ cells from the ovaries. An egg passes through the

_____ to the _____. If a pregnancy occurs, this is where a baby grows and

develops.

B Label the main structures of the female reproductive system on the diagram below.

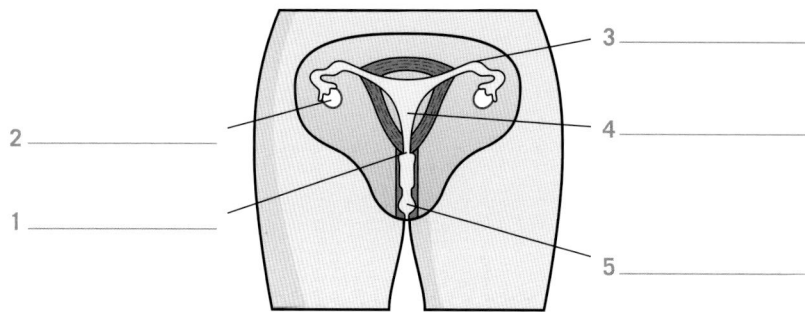

C Label the main structures of the male reproductive system on the diagram below.

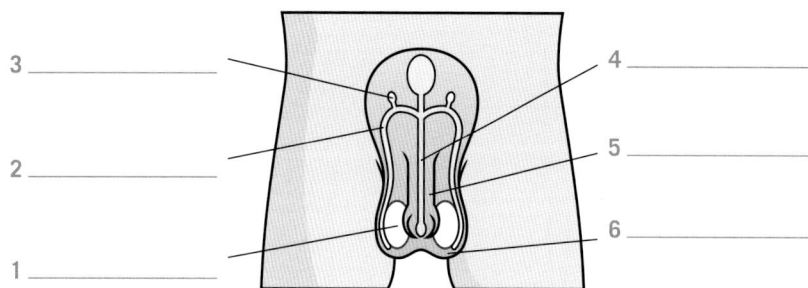

D Describe the function of the following structures.

    a Ovary_____

    b Cervix_____

    c Vagina_____

E Explain how sperm is made and released from the male body.

Include the following terms in your answer:

glands	penis	semen	sperm duct	testicles	urethra

_____

_____

_____

_____

10.2.3 Fertilisation and implantation

A Fill in the gaps to complete the sentences.

Every month an egg is released from an _____ and wafted along the oviduct by tiny hairs

called _____. During sexual intercourse, sperm are released into the vagina. This is known

as _____. The sperm swim towards the egg in the oviduct. To create a new organism the

_____ of the sperm and egg cell need to join together. This is called _____.

The fertilised egg then divides to form a ball of cells called an _____. The embryo

attaches to the lining of the _____ and begins to develop into a baby. This is called

_____.

B Complete the flow diagram to show the structures in the female body that the sperm passes through in order to fertilise an egg.

| Sperm released from penis | → | | → | | → | | → | |

C Describe what happens to the fertilised egg after fertilisation.

_____

_____

_____

D Some couples have difficulty conceiving a child.

a Describe one cause of low fertility in males.

_____

_____

b Describe one cause of low fertility in females.

_____

_____

10.2.4 Development of a fetus

A Fill in the gaps to complete the sentences.

The period of time an organism develops in the _____ is known as _____. In humans

this is about _____ months. The fetus develops inside _____ fluid. This protects

the fetus from any bumps. During this time the fetus receives nutrients and _____ from the

mother. These pass from the mother's blood to the fetus's _____ in the _____. The

fetus is connected to the placenta by the _____ _____. During birth the mother's

_____ relaxes and the _____ wall contracts, pushing the baby out of the body

through the _____.

B Describe briefly what happens during gestation.

_____

_____

C After eight weeks of growth, the embryo is called a fetus. Label the main structures in the diagram below.

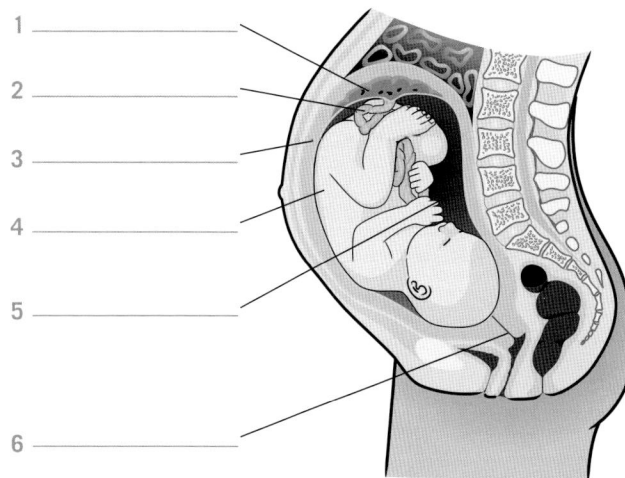

1 _____

2 _____

3 _____

4 _____

5 _____

6 _____

D Explain the function the following structures perform during gestation.

a Placenta

_____

_____

b Amniotic fluid

_____

_____

E With reference to contractions, explain what happens during birth.

_____

_____

_____

10.2.5 The menstrual cycle

A Fill in the gaps to complete the sentences.

The female reproductive system works in a cycle called the _____ cycle. Each month

an _____ is released. This is called _____. If this is not fertilised the uterus

_____ breaks down and leaves the body. This is called a _____. The cycle

then begins again.

B Add labels to the diagram below to indicate when the main events in the menstrual cycle occur.

DAY:	**0 / 1**	**5**	**10**	**15**	**20**	**25**	**28**

C **a** Describe what happens to the uterus lining if the egg is **not** fertilised.

_____

_____

b Describe what happens to the uterus lining if the egg **is** fertilised.

_____

_____

_____

D For **two** named methods of contraception, explain how they prevent pregnancy.

Method 1 _____

Explanation _____

Method 2 _____

Explanation _____

Pinchpoint question

Answer the question below, then do the follow-up activity **with the same letter** as the answer you picked.

Which shape is most suited for absorbing water?

A   Shape A as it has a smaller surface area

B   Shape B as It has a larger surface area

C   Either shape as they have the same surface area

D   Either shape as they have the same volume

4 mm

4 mm

4 mm

Shape A

2 mm

8 mm

4 mm

Shape B

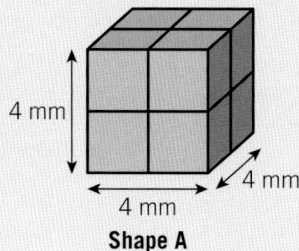

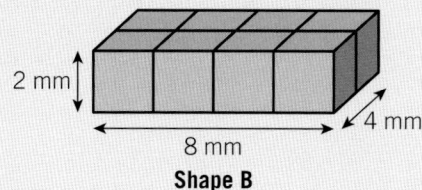

Follow-up activities

A a   Plant roots are adapted to absorb as much water as possible. The water diffuses into the root hair cells from the soil.

Look back at the diagram in the question at the top of this page. Imagine that one molecule of water could diffuse into each surface square of the shape, at the same time.

Use the table to calculate how many molecules of water are diffusing at the same time.

Faces	Shape A	Shape B
Top and bottom	$2 \times 4 = 8$	
Front (facing you) and back		
Left and right		
Total		

Hint: If you find it difficult to visualise the shapes, use a real 3D shape such as your rubber or pencil case to help. For further help see 10.1.3 Adapting to change and 8.2.4 Movement of substances.

b   Explain why Arctic foxes have short ears whereas foxes that live in deserts have large, thin ears.

_____

_____

_____

_____

_____

_____

Arctic fox

Fennec (desert) fox

B   Useful nutrients diffuse into your blood from your small intestine. To maximise this exchange, your small intestine is covered in finger-like projections called villi.

Suggest how villi help the process of nutrient absorption.

Hint: Villi and root hair cells have similar functions. For further help see 10.1.3 Adapting to change and 8.2.4 Movement of substances.

_____

_____

_____

C The surface area of shape A is 96 mm².

   a Calculate the surface area of shape B.

Hint: To calculate the surface area, you need to work out the area of each face of the cuboid by multiplying its length by its width. Then add the area of all the faces together. Some people find it easier to draw out the net of the shape first: you can use the one shown below. For further help see 10.1.3 Adapting to change and 8.2.4 Movement of substances.

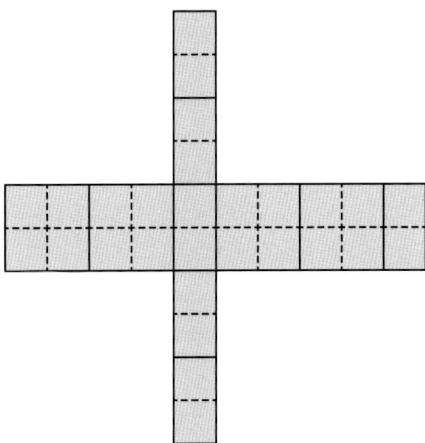

_____ mm²

   b Now complete the following sentence by circling the correct term.

      The surface area of shape B is **bigger than / smaller than / the same as** shape A.

D Water is placed into two containers, A and B, which have the same volume. Container A represents a narrow, deep puddle and container B represents a shallow, wide puddle. They are placed outside on a sunny day.

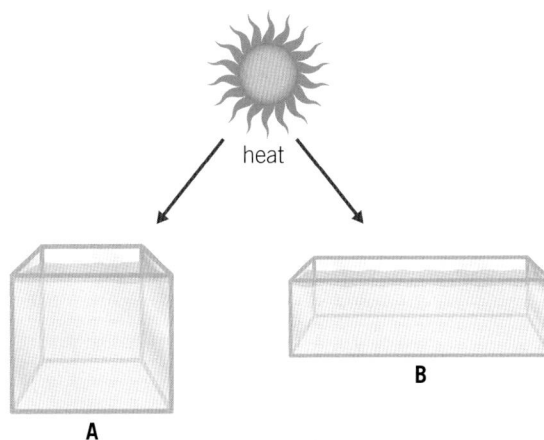

Complete the following sentences by circling the correct term in each sentence.

As the Sun shines on the puddle, the water will **diffuse / condense / evaporate**.

The surface area of container A exposed to the Sun is **the same as / larger than / smaller than** that of container B.

Therefore puddle **A / B** will disappear faster even though they have the same volume.

Hint: Think about which puddle will be affected most by the heat from the Sun. For further help see 10.1.3 Adapting to change and 8.2.4 Movement of substances.

> ### Pinchpoint review
> Now look back at the question – do you think you chose the right letter?
> Turn to the Answers page to find out.

Section 3 Revision questions

1 ⚗⚗ **Figure 1** shows a flower.

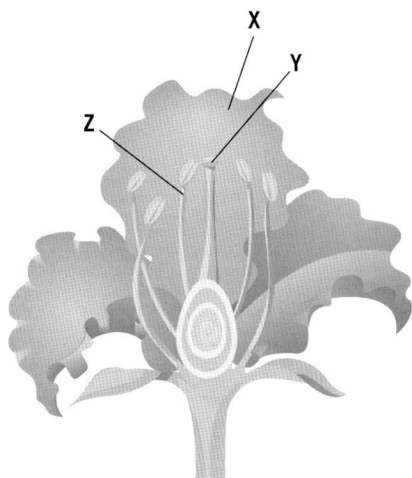

Figure 1

a Name the structures **X**, **Y**, and **Z**. *(3 marks)*

X _____

Y _____

Z _____

b Pollen and ovules are the plant gametes.

   i Define the word **gamete**. *(1 mark)*

_____

   ii Name the part of the flower where pollen is made.
(1 mark)

_____

   iii Name the part of the flower where ovules are found. *(1 mark)*

_____

c Give **two** different ways in which a plant can be pollinated and give an example of a plant which is pollinated by each method. *(2 marks)*

   1 _____ example: _____

   2 _____ example: _____

d To produce a seed, fertilisation must occur.

Describe what happens during the process of fertilisation. *(2 marks)*

_____

_____

_____

2 ⚗⚗ Plant and animal cells contain smaller structures.

a Draw a line from each plant cell structure to its correct function. *(3 marks)*

nucleus	stores sap and helps to keep the cell firm
vacuole	controls the activities of the cell
cytoplasm	where the cell's chemical reactions take place

b Explain why plant cells contain chloroplasts.
(1 mark)

_____

_____

3 ⚗⚗ A group of students wanted to observe some onion cells under a microscope.

a Explain how the students should set up and use the microscope so they can view the cells clearly.
(6 marks)

_____

_____

_____

_____

_____

_____

_____

_____

_____

_____

b Sketch a diagram below, showing what you would expect the students to see through the microscope. Label **three** cell components.
(4 marks)

c Plant cells have a cell wall.

   i Write down what cell walls are made from.
(1 mark)

_____

ii Explain the function of the cell wall. (*2 marks*)

_____

_____

4 🧪🧪 Hermione measured the force of her triceps muscle by pushing down onto a set of bathroom scales, measuring the force in newtons. **Table 1** shows her results.

Table 1

Force measurement 1 (N)	Force measurement 2 (N)	Force measurement 3 (N)
450	410	370

a Calculate the mean force from Hermione's triceps muscle. Remember to state the units. (*3 marks*)

_____

b Suggest **one** reason why each force measurement was different. (*1 mark*)

_____

_____

c The biceps and triceps muscles are found in the upper arm, as shown in **Figure 2**.

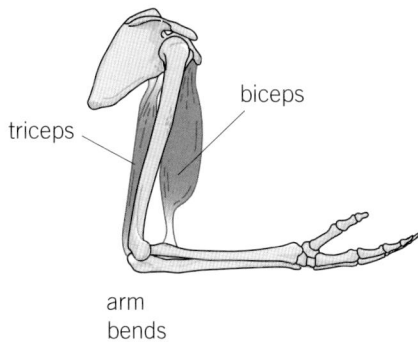

biceps

triceps

arm bends

Figure 2

Explain how these muscles work together to move your lower arm upwards and downwards.
(*3 marks*)

_____

_____

_____

_____

5 🧪🧪 Basil is an edible plant. A group of students were asked to investigate the conditions needed for basil seeds to germinate. They placed seeds onto cotton wool, in the conditions shown in **Figure 3**.

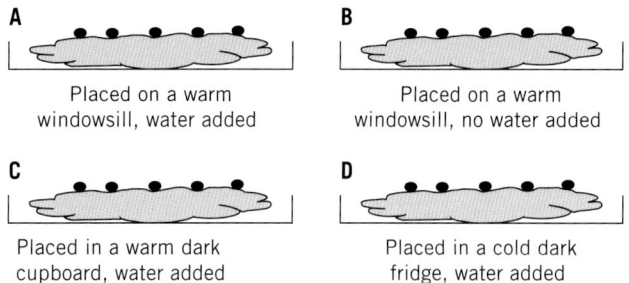

A
Placed on a warm windowsill, water added

B
Placed on a warm windowsill, no water added

C
Placed in a warm dark cupboard, water added

D
Placed in a cold dark fridge, water added

Figure 3

a Circle each dish where you would expect germination to occur. (*2 marks*)

b The students used a total of 20 seeds. Only 8 of these germinated.

Calculate the percentage of seeds that germinated.
(*2 marks*)

_____%

c Basil seeds have a sticky outer layer, called mucilage. Suggest and explain how basil seeds are dispersed. (*2 marks*)

_____

_____

_____

_____

6 🧪🧪🧪 A couple wish to have a baby.

a When is the most likely time in a woman's menstrual cycle for her to get pregnant?

Days 1 → 3 ☐   Days 14 → 16 ☐

Days 24 → 26 ☐ (*1 mark*)

b Explain your answer. (*2 marks*)

_____

_____

c Explain how sexual intercourse can lead to a fertilised egg implanting in the uterus. *(6 marks)*

_____

_____

_____

_____

_____

_____

_____

7 ⚗⚗⚗ **Figure 4** shows a drawing of a flower.

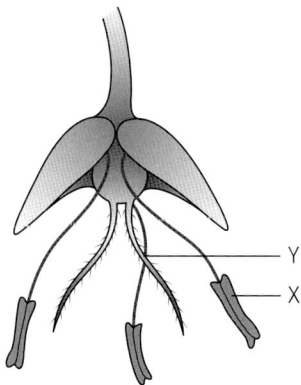

Figure 4

a Identify structures X and Y.

X _____ *(1 mark)*

Y _____ *(1 mark)*

b Use information in the diagram and your own knowledge to explain how this flower is pollinated. *(4 marks)*

_____

_____

_____

_____

_____

8 ⚗⚗⚗ A group of students observed some pond-water organisms under the microscope. They placed a droplet of water containing *Daphnia* on a special slide, as shown in **Figure 5**.

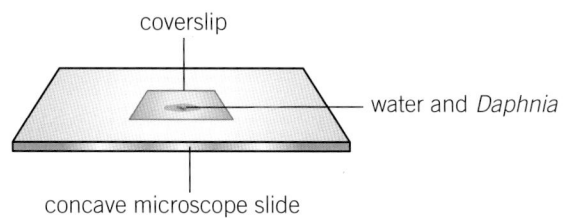

Figure 5

a Suggest **one** reason why they added water. *(1 mark)*

_____

b **Figure 6** shows what they observed using a ×10 eyepiece lens and a ×4 objective lens.

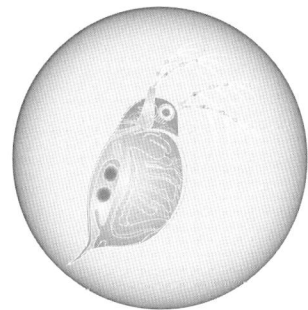

Figure 6

i Calculate the total magnification used. *(1 mark)*

_____ %

ii Use information in the diagram to explain how the students knew they were looking at a multicellular organism. *(2 marks)*

_____

_____

_____

c The students could see the heart of the *Daphnia* beating.

i Explain how they could observe the heart in more detail. *(1 mark)*

_____

ii Name **one** type of specialised cell they would expect to find in this organ and explain its function. *(2 marks)*

_____

_____

Section 3 Checklist

Revision question	Outcome	Topic reference	🙁	😐	🙂
1a	Identify the main structures in a flower.	9.2.1			
1b	State the definition of 'gamete'. State the function of parts of a flower.	9.2.1 10.2.2			
1c	Name two different ways in which a plant can be pollinated.	9.2.1			
1d	Describe the process of fertilisation.	9.2.2			
2a	Match some components of a cell to their functions.	8.2.2			
2b	State the function of chloroplasts.	8.2.2			
3a	Describe how to use a microscope to observe a cell.	8.2.1			
3b	Sketch a plant cell as it would appear through a microscope.	8.2.2			
3c	Describe the function of cell components.	8.2.2			
4a	Calculate a mean average.	EP3 8.1.4			
4b	Suggest reasons for variation in experimental data.	EP5			
4c	Explain how muscles work together to produce movement.	8.1.4			
5a	Describe the conditions required for seed germination.	9.2.2			
5b	Calculate a percentage from experimental data.	9.2.2			
5c	Describe methods of seed dispersal.	9.2.3			
6a, b	Describe the stages of the menstrual cycle.	10.2.5			
6c	Explain how the male and female reproductive systems work together to result in pregnancy.	10.2.3			
7a	Identify the main structures in an unknown flower.	9.2.1			
7b	Explain how the structures in a flower are adapted for pollination.	9.2.1			
8a	Select appropriate experimental apparatus.	EP2			
8bi	Calculate magnification used to observe an organism.	8.2.1			
8bii	Explain what a unicellular organism is.	8.2.5			
8ci	Explain how to use a microscope to observe structures in more detail.	8.2.1			
8cii	Describe examples of specialised animal cells.	8.2.3			

Answers

EP1 and EP2

A question, prediction, knowledge, independent, dependent, control, equipment, risk assessment, data, precise

B **a** the variable you change

  b the variable that changes because of the variable you change

  c a variable that must be kept the same during an investigation

C pattern seeking enquiry

D data, accurate, precise, repeatable

E C

F **one** from: risk of burns – handle with tongs; risk of sparks – wear eye protection; risk of damage to eyes (extreme brightness) – observe burning metal through filter / darkened screen

EP3

A results, independent, measurements / readings / observations, mean, units, outliers, repeat, scale, x, line graph, bar chart, pie chart

B

Angle (degrees)	Distance 1 (cm)	Distance 2 (cm)	Distance 3 (cm)	Mean distance (cm)

C 80 cm

D $\dfrac{48 + 50 + 55}{3} = 51$ cm

E x-axis – angle of slope (degrees); y-axis – mean distance travelled (cm); linear scales, must start at zero for both axes, x-axis should not exceed 40°; points plotted at approximately (20, 51), (30, 59) and at (0, 0); (positive correlation)

EP4

A data, best fit, curve, conclusion, relationship, scientific, prediction

B as temperature increases, time to dissolve decreases; when temperature doubles, the time to dissolve reduces by less than half

C **a** the point at (6.0, 3.8) should be labelled as an outlier; the best-fit line should only use the other seven points

  b the prediction was correct; more specifically, extension is proportional to force – as force doubles, so does extension; the measurement of extension when force is 6 N is an outlier, far from the trend in the data; it appears to be a mistake; I have not used it to draw the best-fit line

EP5

A evaluate, quality, data, improvements, method, confidence, outliers, precise, more, random, systematic, range, more / repeat

B discuss the quality of the data you have collected; suggest and explain improvements to your method so you can collect data of better quality if you do it again

C **a** both groups have similar averages, so have similar accuracy; group 1 has a larger spread of readings than group 2; group 1 might have been less careful, or used a less precise measurement instrument, or it could just be random; group 2 has a larger number of readings than group 1

  b **two** from: take more repeat readings to detect outliers; set up their equipment and take readings more carefully in case they were not using the equipment as well as possible; use a more precise measuring instrument in case that reduces the spread of the results

Enquiry Processes Pinchpoint

A this is an incorrect answer – changing variables will **not** improve confidence in the conclusion

B this is an incorrect answer – repetition of readings lets you know the precision of the result; you reduce uncertainty by improving or changing the measuring instrument

C this is the correct answer

D this is an incorrect answer – you need to find ways to **decrease**, not increase, the spread to improve precision

Pinchpoint follow-up

A accurate – close to the true value of what you are measuring; precise – this describes a set of repeat measurements that are close together; repeatable – when you take the measurements of an investigation again and get similar results; reproducible – when other people carry out the same investigation and get similar measurements

B **accuracy**: 1, 3, 4; **precision**: 2, 5

C **a** **two** from: different-sized bubbles, too fast to count, might miss some

  b collect gas in a small measuring cylinder or gas syringe to measure the volume of gas (or other suitable suggestion)

D 2, 4, 5

1.1.1

A push, pull (either order), move, direction, shape, gravity, friction / air resistance, air resistance / friction, interaction, measured, newtons / N

B A force of friction of the road on the tyre makes a bus change speed. A force of air resistance of the air on their parachute helps a skydiver land safely. A force of gravity of the Earth on the water makes spilt water spread into a puddle.

C every force is the result of the interaction of two different objects; for air resistance, the object affected must be touching the air molecules; for gravity, the object affected does not need to touch the object causing the gravitational force

D a

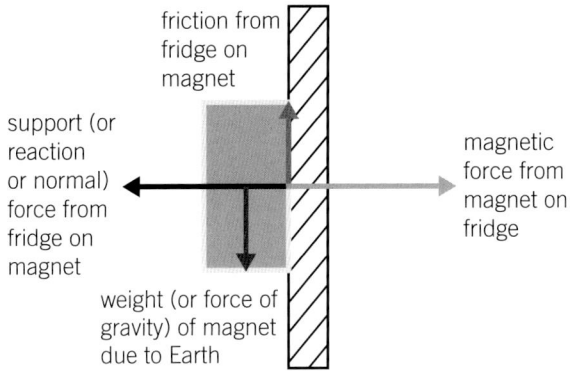

friction from fridge on magnet

support (or reaction or normal) force from fridge on magnet

magnetic force from magnet on fridge

weight (or force of gravity) of magnet due to Earth

b (weight of magnet due to Earth) weight (or force of gravity) of Earth due to magnet; (friction from fridge on magnet) friction from magnet on fridge; (support force from fridge on magnet) support (or reaction or normal) force from magnet on fridge; (magnetic force from fridge on magnet) magnetic force from magnet on fridge

1.1.2

A push, pull, move, direction, shape, gravity, friction / air resistance, air resistance / friction, interaction, measured, newtons / N

B **two** from: aeroplane at constant speed (thrust equal and opposite to air resistance); person floating in swimming pool (weight equal and opposite to upthrust); cup on table (support force equal and opposite to weight); any other suitable answer; **not**, e.g., bike speeding up / slowing down / turning corner, Moon orbiting Earth

C a any combination showing equal arrows going in opposite direction, such as one each up and down, or left and right

b any combination showing unequal arrows in opposite direction, such as up, down, left but not right; or with at least one arrow not of equal length to the others

c balanced forces are when there are pairs of forces on an object that are equal but in opposite directions so they cancel out, e.g. when the bus is stationary; unbalanced means there is a force that is not cancelled, e.g. when the bus speeds up, the driving force is larger than the resistive forces

D only one force is acting on the Moon, so the resultant force is towards the Earth; the Moon keeps changing direction towards the Earth

1.1.3

A speed, distance, metre(s) per second, distance, speed, speed, instantaneous speed, average speed, relative motion, relative speed, relative speed

B a $\frac{160}{2.0} = 80\,\text{km/h}$ (to 2 sig. fig.)

b $\frac{500}{30} = 17\,\text{m/s}$ (to 2 sig. fig.)

c $330 \times 12 = 4000\,\text{m}$ (to 2 sig. fig.)

C a $\text{speed} = \frac{\text{distance}}{\text{time}} = \frac{20\,\text{m}}{0.5\,\text{s}} = 40\,\text{m/s}$

b yes, it was breaking the speed limit

D a appears to be moving quickly

b appears to be stationary

1.1.4

A distance–time, horizontal, speed, accelerating

B a i 0.00; 0.04; 0.12; 0.28; 0.44; 0.60; 0.76; 0.80; 0.81

ii

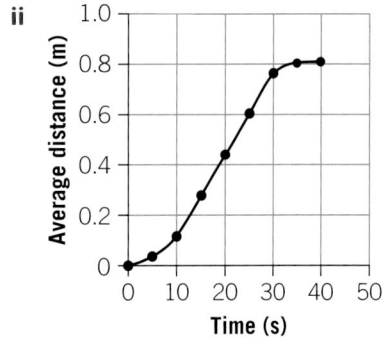

b i the toy starts stationary; it accelerates for 10 s

ii it moves at its fastest, constant speed for 20 s

iii it then slows to a stop in 10 s

c speed = 0.032 m/s (to 2 sig. fig.)

1.2.1

A fields, non-contact, charge, charge, stronger, gravitational, decreases, gravity, mass

B a force, masses, gets weaker

C Earth's surface – 1600; orbit – 1400; Moon's surface – 260 (to 2 sig. fig.); far from any star or planet – 0

D a nearer to charges in cloud, so stronger field; more likely to be struck by lightning

b similarity – **one** from: cause forces, weaker with distance, stronger with increasing mass or charge; difference – electrical affects charge but gravitational affects mass

E the gravitational force is a pull towards the Earth; it is low and keeps decreasing; gravity is a non-contact force – a field – which is why the probe still has this force on it; the field weakens with distance, which is why the force keeps decreasing

Big Idea 1 Pinchpoint

A this is an incorrect answer: there must be an **unbalanced** force to cause a turn but the diagram and statement show balanced forces

B this is the correct answer

C this is an incorrect answer: it correctly states that the forces are unbalanced but the diagram wrongly shows **balanced** forces

D this is an incorrect answer: the diagram is correct but the forces are **not** balanced

Pinchpoint follow-up

A a i one arrow up from centre of ball labelled 'support force from hand', second arrow same size, down from centre of ball, labelled 'force of gravity from Earth' (or just 'weight')

        ii yes   **iii** no (it remains stationary)
  b **i**   a single arrow down from centre of ball, labelled
            'force of gravity from Earth' (or just 'weight')
        ii no   **iii** yes (it is speeding up, towards ground)
B **a** arrow drawn from centre of cyclist pointing to right
        (towards centre of the circle)
  b arrow drawn from centre of cyclist pointing down
        (towards centre of the circle)
C **a** cyclist pushing road to the left
  b arrow from box where their hands touch it, to the right,
        equal in size to the left arrow
  c the person
D **a** unbalanced, change, right **b** balanced, not change

2.1.1

A cell, battery (either order), potential difference, voltmeter,
    parallel, volts, V, voltage, rating, high / large, energy,
    low / small

B **a** **b** cell, voltage, cell, volts

C current – same – charge; p.d. – total – energy
D **a** gets dimmer / goes out **b** gets brighter / burns out
E ammeter measures the current passing through it so needs
    to be in the path of the current, that is 'in series'; voltmeter
    measures the amount of energy transferred between
    two points, so is connected across those two points or 'in
    parallel' with them

2.1.2

A resistance, potential difference, current, ohm, resistance,
    high, low

B $\dfrac{6.0}{0.20} = 30\ \Omega$

C **a** $\text{current (A)} = \dfrac{\text{potential difference (V)}}{\text{resistance }(\Omega)}$

  b $\dfrac{9.0}{30} = 0.30\ \text{A}$

D **a** potential difference (V) = current (A) × resistance (Ω)
  b 0.50 × 20 = 10 V
E moving electrons (charges) colliding with vibrating metal
    ions (atoms) as they pass along the wire
F length – increases – more vibrating particles;
    diameter – decreases – more paths
G resistance of coating is greater than resistance of wire; wire
    needs to allow charges to pass / current to flow; coating
    must not let current flow or person get shock

2.1.3

A series, potential difference, potential difference, parallel,
    potential difference

B **a** 6 V   **b** 6 V
C increases
D series – amount of energy transferred into a circuit by the cell
    equals the total amount of energy transferred into the
    components, so the total p.d. across the components must
    add up to the p.d. across the cell; parallel – a charge passes
    through only one of the branches at a time and the amount
    of energy transferred into a circuit by a cell must equal the
    amount of energy transferred into any one branch, so the p.d.
    across each branch must be the same as that across the cell

2.2.1

A electrons, second, ammeter, series, ammeter, amp, A, motor,
    switch, complete

B **a**   **b** series

  c movement of charge (or charged particles); amount of
        charge flowing per second
C **a** decreases   **b** 0.8 A
D **a** **i** charge   **ii** the speed of the rope
  b same number of charges in the circuit, but they are now
        moving more slowly

2.2.2

A protons, electrons, neutral, friction, electrons, negatively,
    electric field, electrostatic, repel, attract, lightning
B **a** friction, electrons, electrons, positive, negative
  b A – repel; B – attract; C – attract; D – repel
C **a** paint droplets lose electrons
  b **i** paint droplets attracted to car
        ii more paint adheres to the car / less paint is wasted
D friction between clothes and seat charges car and person;
    person touches metal door while standing on ground, so
    electrons flow, causing a shock

Big Idea 2 Pinchpoint

A this is an incorrect answer – current is **not** 'used up' by
    components
B this is an incorrect answer – the bulbs are **dimmer** in the
    series circuit because it has higher resistance
C this is an incorrect answer – the potential difference across
    each bulb in the parallel circuit is the **same** as that of the
    cell, whereas the p.d. across the cell is **split** between the
    two bulbs in the series circuit
D this is the correct answer

Pinchpoint follow-up

A created, destroyed, same, flowing, second, same, current
B **a** increase **b** decrease **c** lower **d** same
C **a** a measure of the push of a cell or battery, or the energy
        that the cell or battery can supply
  b **i** potential difference tells you how much energy can
            be transferred to a circuit

ii the potential difference across all branches of a parallel circuit must be the same

iii any one electron must do the same work on the components as the battery did on it

iv the p.d. across each branch in a circuit is always equal to the p.d. across the cell

D **a** 1.5V; parallel circuit so 3.0V across each branch, two identical components in series, so same p.d. across each so they add up to 3.0V

b 0.6A; parallel circuit so current through both branches together must add up to 1.2A; branches are identical, so same current through each branch; as the two bulbs in each branch are in series, the current is the same through each bulb

3.1.1

A energy, joule, kilojoule, activities, fat

B **a** sleeping 300; working 600; running 3600

b sleeping involves no exercise but running involves a lot, so requires more energy

C **a** $20 \times 300 = 6000\,\text{kJ}$

b anything that adds up to previous answer, e.g. 400g of chicken breast, 400g of pasta, 100g of banana, 110g of apple

c **i** $300 \times \dfrac{160}{2} = 24\,000\,\text{kJ}$

ii 1.3kg of dried fruit & nut mix or 1.6kg of chocolate

D walking: $1 \times 800 = 800$; working: $6 \times 600 = 3600$; relaxing: $5 \times 360 = 1800$; sleeping: $12 \times 300 = 3600$; total: 9800kJ

3.1.2

A energy resource, fossil fuels, non-renewable, renewable, carbon dioxide, sulfur dioxide

B **a** natural gas, biogas **b** 2, 5, 1, 4, 6, 3

C e.g. renewables – will never run out; do not produce greenhouse gases; do not contribute to global warming; do not produce acid rain; produce little waste; need no 'fuel' so cheap to run; non-renewables – historically tended to be cheaper; a lot of energy per kg of fuel; reliable

D reduce demand for electricity, which means burning less fossil fuel; build more renewable or nuclear power stations, which do not burn fossil fuels and so reduce production of carbon dioxide

3.1.3

A energy, time, energy, power, current, potential difference (either order), power rating, watt, kilowatt, kilowatt hour

B **a** $\dfrac{45\,000}{30} = 1500\,\text{W}$

b **i** $10 \times 230 = 2300\,\text{W}$

ii $2300 \times 30 = 69\,000\,\text{J or 69 kJ}$

c $2 \times 4 = 8\,\text{kWh}$

C **a** cost = power × time × cost per unit

$= \dfrac{75}{1000} \times (4 \times 365) \times 15 = 1643\,\text{p}$

b cost = power × time × cost per unit

$= \dfrac{11}{1000} \times (4 \times 365) \times 15 = 241\,\text{p}$

c £16.43 – £2.41 = £14.02

3.2.1

A conservation, energy, energy stores, fill, total, chemical, thermal, kinetic, gravitational potential, elastic

B **a** chemical store – coal fuel (and oxygen in air); thermal store – water; thermal store – surroundings

b chemical store – fuel in car (and oxygen in air); kinetic store – car; thermal store – car and surroundings

c gravitational potential store – Charlie and scooter; kinetic store – Charlie and scooter; thermal store – scooter wheels and ground

C **a** **i** gravitational store of skier, fills; chemical store of fuel, empties; thermal store of surroundings, fills

ii thermal store of surroundings

b **i** power station transfers energy to the lift using electrical current

ii chemical store of coal empties by as much as the gravitational store of the lift and people fills

D left lid off saucepan – systematic – put lid on; thermometer reading – random – read thermometer at eye level each time; timing – random – repeat experiment three times

3.2.2

A dissipated, thermal, thermal

B **a** **i** 2 **ii** 3 **iii** 1

b when electricity does work on the toaster, it heats the toast but also heats the surroundings; the energy transferred to the thermal energy store of the surroundings has dissipated and cannot easily be used for anything else

C **a** **i** $9.0 - 8.2 = 0.8\,\text{W}$

ii efficiency $= \dfrac{\text{useful power output}}{\text{power input}} \times 100$

$= \dfrac{0.8}{9.0} = 8.9\%$

b **i** $3 \times 2000 = 6000\,\text{J}$

ii efficiency $= \dfrac{\text{useful power output}}{\text{power input}} \times 100$;

$\dfrac{2000}{(2000 + 6000)} \times 100 = \dfrac{2000}{8000} \times 100 = 25\%$

D burning it in a power station – better efficiency means less lost via dissipation

Big Idea 3 Pinchpoint

A this is an incorrect answer – a store of energy cannot just be 'used up'

B this is the correct answer

C this is an incorrect answer – the battery does not store electricity, it has a store of **chemical energy**

D this is an incorrect answer – the thermal energy store of the room **does not increase**; it **empties and fills at the same rate** so that it stays constant; it is the increase in the thermal store of the **surroundings** that is equal to the loss from the chemical store

Pinchpoint follow-up

A **a** warmer, heated, empties, fills, fill
   b constant, empties, rate, fills, warmer
B increases temperature difference between inside of house and surroundings; house heats surroundings faster; over one hour, thermal store of surroundings fills more
C work, store, chemical, fuel, thermal, water, chemical, fuel, chemical, dissipation, surroundings
D **a** true   **b** false   **c** true
   d false   **e** true   **f** true

4.1.1

A vibrate, particles / molecules, vacuum, solid, quickly, light, medium
B sound waves travel faster in solids than gases; particles in a solid are very close together, so the vibration is passed along more quickly than in a gas
C travelling faster than the speed of sound
D light travels much faster than sound, so light takes much less time to travel the same distance; the observer sees the explosion almost immediately, but hears it after a delay
E sound is the transfer of energy through vibrations of particles; space is a vacuum, where there are no particles, so sound cannot travel through it

4.1.2

A peak, crest, trough, middle, top, wavelength, waves, second, oscillation, parallel, oscilloscope, absorbed, reflected, echo

B oscillations parallel to wave motion

C **a** larger amplitude, for example:

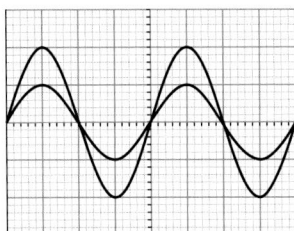

   b **i** use an oscilloscope; measure distance from centre of wave to trough or crest
      ii $2 \times 4\,V = 8.0\,V$
D the loud sound in the neighbour's house causes the particles in the wall to vibrate forwards and backwards, within the wall; as the sound wave passes out of the other side, the surface wall particles push against the

nearest air particles, which then start vibrating forwards and backwards, passing on the vibration to neighbouring particles and transmitting the sound as a longitudinal wave

4.1.3

A frequency, hertz, kilohertz, frequency, 20, infrasound, frequency, 20 000, ultrasound, audible
B **a** arrow from one peak to next peak (or trough to trough or zero-crossing to zero-crossing)

   b $4 \times \dfrac{5}{1000} = 0.020\,s$ **c** $\dfrac{1}{0.020} = 50\,Hz$

C longer period, for example:

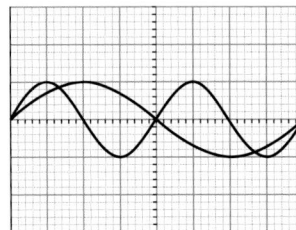

D human – hear a sound – within hearing range;
   bat – hear nothing – below hearing range;
   dog – hear a sound – within hearing range

4.1.4

A ear, pinna, auditory, eardrum, ossicles, amplify, cochlea, hair, nerve, brain, volume, decibels, damage
B 5, 3, 1, 2, 6, 7, 8, 4
C **a** pneumatic drills are very loud; ear defenders reduce sound intensity; loud noises damage sensitive cells at base of hairs in the cochlea; damage can be temporary or permanent, but the risk of permanent damage increases the louder the noise is
   b ten times louder
D the foam in our ear defenders **absorbs** most of the sound wave; this ensures that the amplitude of the transmitted wave is **small** so that **little** power reaches the user's ears

4.2.1

A luminous, source, non-luminous, reflected, eye, transmit, opaque, translucent, scattered, Sun, Earth, (either order) umbra, total solar, penumbra, partial solar, Moon, lunar
B 4, 5, 1, 3, 2 (or 1, 3, 4, 5, 2)
C **a**

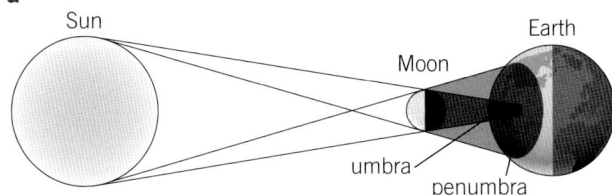

   b in the penumbra, as part of the Sun's light is blocked by the Moon
D **a** cat – some reflected and some absorbed
   b glass – transmitted   **c** eye – absorbed

4.2.2

A reflects, reflects, incident, reflected, normal, equal, incidence, reflection, plane, specular, virtual, scattered, diffuse

B **a** angle of reflection = angle of incidence (or both angles are the same / equal)

   b diffuse scattering

   c the light rays striking the surface are parallel; however, because the surface is rough, the angle of incidence is different in different places, so the angle of reflection is different

C

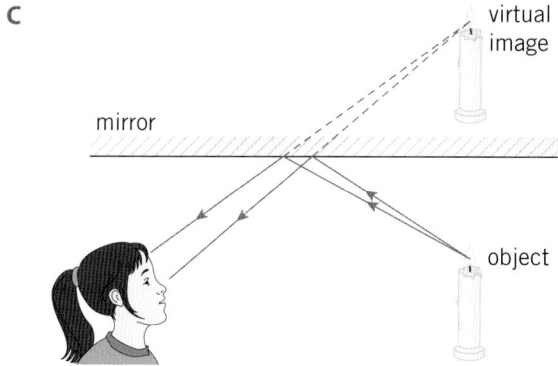

D **a** walls and floor of room are not perfectly smooth; sunlight falls on them and scatters off diffusely, at lots of different angles; some of this enters your eye, making the room appear bright

   b things like metal panels on car and shop windows are very smooth; sunlight falls on them and undergoes specular reflection; sometimes when you are in a particular spot you then see the image of the Sun reflected, which is very bright

4.2.3

A medium, speed, direction, refraction, slows down, towards, shallower / less deep, converging, focus, converging, real, virtual

B **a** light reflects from the stone and travels up through the water; when it passes into the air it changes speed – slower in the water, faster in the air; this causes the ray of light to bend (away from the normal), called refraction

   b

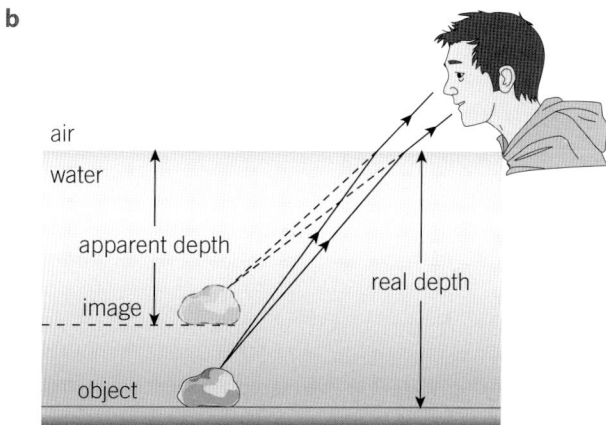

C **a**

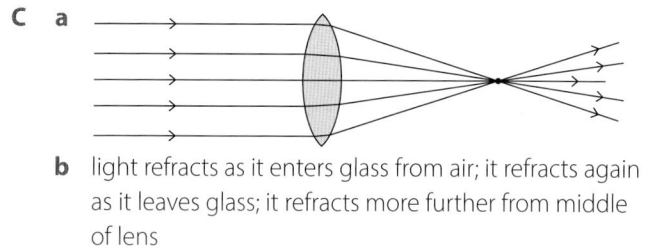

   b light refracts as it enters glass from air; it refracts again as it leaves glass; it refracts more further from middle of lens

4.2.4

A focusing, object, lens, iris, pupil, retina, photoreceptors, chemical, optic

B object – reflected light from this enters the eye; cornea and lens – focus the light; iris – controls the size of the pupil, allowing in more or less light; pupil – a hole that allows light to enter the lens; retina – where the image forms – contains photoreceptors; photoreceptors – rods and cones – absorb light causing a chemical reaction which produces an electrical signal; image – real (you could put a screen here and you would see an image), inverted, smaller than the object; optic nerve – sends electrical signal to the brain

C light refracts as it passes through the cornea and lens; bends rays to focus them at back of the eye on the retina; pupil allows light to enter; real image; image is inverted; image is smaller than object

D eyeball too long / lens–cornea combination refracting light too much; concave lens used; diverges light rays to reach retina

4.2.5

A primary, secondary, cyan, primary, white, subtract, subtracts, blue, reflecting, blue, prism, spectrum, dispersion, frequency, lowest, continuous

B light refracts as it enters and leaves glass of the prism; white light consists of light of many different wavelengths / frequencies / colours; different wavelengths of light refract by different amounts, this is called dispersion; violet refracts more than red

C primary red added to primary green; our eyes absorb that light, detecting both red and green; we perceive that as the secondary colour yellow

D **a** it will appear black; white reflects all colours, so the red light is reflected to the filter; green filters absorb all colours except green, so no red light is transmitted through the filter, and no light reaches the eye, so the object appears black

   b it will appear green; white light consists of all colours, including green; green objects reflect green light and absorb all others, so green light is reflected to the filter; green filters transmit green light, so the green light reaches the eye

E the ball will appear red; secondary yellow light consists of red and green light; the red ball absorbs all colours except red, so it absorbs the green light, leaving the red light to reflect and be detected by the eye

Big Idea 4 Pinchpoint

A this is an incorrect answer – the ray must bend **away from** the normal as it leaves the glass

B this is the correct answer

C this is an incorrect answer – it shows the ray being **absorbed** when it reaches the edge of the glass, instead of **refracting** into the air

D this is an incorrect answer – it shows the ray **reflecting** inside the glass, instead of **refracting** into the air

Pinchpoint follow-up

A **a** slower

   b light **refracts** (or bends or deflects) **towards** the **normal** when going from a **medium** in which it travels **faster** into one where it is **slower**; it refracts **away** from the normal when passing from **slower** into **faster**

B the bottom of the spoon appears in a different place from the top because light reflected from the spoon through the water refracts as it leaves the water; bottom of spoon appears larger because curved container means water acts as a lens

C absorbed, scattered, transmitted, refract, normal, faster, slower, slower, faster

D **a** mirror, reflected, transmitted, refracts, towards, slows down, away from, speeds up

   b **i** reflected ray going down to right at same angle as incoming ray

   ii refracted ray inside glass going up to right at angle nearer to normal

Section 1 Revision questions

1 **a** gravity [1]

   b **either**: drag (air resistance) from air on parachute [1] and drag from parachute on air [1]; **or** weight (force of gravity) of skydiver due to Earth [1] and weight of Earth due to skydiver [1]; reason: same type of force [1], same pair of objects [1]

2 particles (molecules) in a liquid / water are closer together than in a gas / air [1]; vibration passed along more quickly [1]

3 **two** from: sharp object puncturing the eardrum [1]; build-up of ear wax [1]; very loud sounds [1]; head injuries [1]

4 **a** add (or mix) green [1] and blue [1]

   b red – no [1]; green – yes – green [1]; blue – no [1]

5 **a** charge [1]   **b** $\frac{12}{4.0} = 3.0$ [1] Ω [1]

   c wire – conductor [1]; wrapping – insulator [1]

6 **a** $\frac{1200}{20} = 60$ [1] W [1]

   b **i** $\frac{60}{1000} = 0.06$ (kW) [1]

   ii cost (p) = power (kW) × time (h) × cost per unit (p / kWh) [1]

   $= 0.06 \times 2 \times 15$ [1] $= 1.8$ p [1]

7 **a** standing still / stationary / not moving [1]

b axes with reasonable scales (time on x-axis, distance on y-axis) [1], accurately plotted points [1], joined point-to-point with straight lines: straight diagonal line from 0 s, 0 m up to 120 s, 180 m; horizontal line across to 180 s, 180 m; straight diagonal line up to 300 s, 280 m [1]

c speed $= \frac{\text{distance}}{\text{time}} = \frac{180}{120}$ [1] $= 1.5$ [1] m/s [1]

8 larger [1], doing more work / exercise [1]

9 **a** **two** different transparent media, e.g. light entering glass from air [1]; ray bends towards the normal as it enters denser medium (or converse) [1]

   b light slows down when entering denser medium, e.g. glass (or converse) [1]

   c rays change direction at lens [1]; all rays pass through focus [1]

   d as power increases, focal length decreases [1]; focal length changes a lot for small powers (or converse) [1]; the point at 7 cm does not fit trend – it is an outlier / anomaly [1]

10 **a** gravity's effect is strongest while on Earth's surface [1]; gets weaker the further away the probe gets [1]; weight of probe changes but mass stays the same [1]

   b x-axis labelled force (kN); y-axis labelled (m/s²) [1]; plotted data [1]; straight line of best fit passing very near origin, diagonally up to very near (5, 73) [1]

11 two waves with same period (number of waves / distance between peaks / troughs) [1] but one with higher amplitude [1]; wave with higher amplitude labelled 'louder' [1]

12 **four** from: glass – refract [1], transmit [1], some light reflected [1]; ball – most colours of light absorbed [1], some light reflected [1], blue light reflected [1]

13 **six** from: natural gas non-renewable [1], can run out [1], produces cheaper electricity [1] (or converse), emits carbon dioxide when used [1] which causes climate change / global warming [1]; wind renewable [1], cannot run out [1], not available all the time / unreliable [1], wind turbines noisy / unsightly [1]

14 **a** electricity charged according to energy transferred [1]; energy transferred is power times time [1]; time to boil more powerful kettle is **less** than half [1]; although power doubled, bill will decrease slightly [1] **or** equivalent numeric argument: (3000 × 140) (J) < (1500 × 300) (J) [1]

   b no [1]; 'best' is not a scientific term – it means different things to different people [1]

15 **a** when she walks, there is friction between shoes and carpet, transferring some electrons to her shoes [1]; this leaves her with negative charge and carpet with positive charge carpet [1]; metal is a conductor [1]; when she touches door handle, electrons flow from her to Earth [1], the electron flow (or current) passing through her is the shock [1]

   b **one** from: different material in carpet / shoe / door [1]; less sensitive to feeling of electricity [1]

5.1.1

A particles, different, looks, behaves, arranged, move

B **a** a gold particle is the same size as a silver particle, and the particles in gold and silver are arranged in the same way; but a gold particle has a greater mass than a silver particle, so gold has a greater density than silver

 b hafnium

C **a** the student can pour the spheres out of each beaker

 b the spheres that represent gold have a greater mass than the spheres that represent silver

 c the particles of gold and silver have different colours and different masses

 d the particles are much bigger and heavier in the model than in reality

5.1.2

A gas(eous), matter, movement, different

B gas; liquid and gas; solid; solid

C **a** its particles are in fixed positions

 b the particles touch their neighbours / the particles cannot get closer together

 c the particles move throughout the container

D good points – particles are arranged randomly, and in the bottom of the container; bad point – the particles are not touching each other

E **a** Brooke

 b each individual grain of sand is solid, and you cannot pour one grain of sand, so it is solid

5.1.3

A melting, faster, away, melting, pure, freezing, slowly

B **a** nine particles, arranged in rows

 b in the liquid, the particles move in all directions, sliding over each other; in the solid, the particles vibrate on the spot / about fixed points; energy from the particles is transferred to the surroundings as the liquid freezes

C

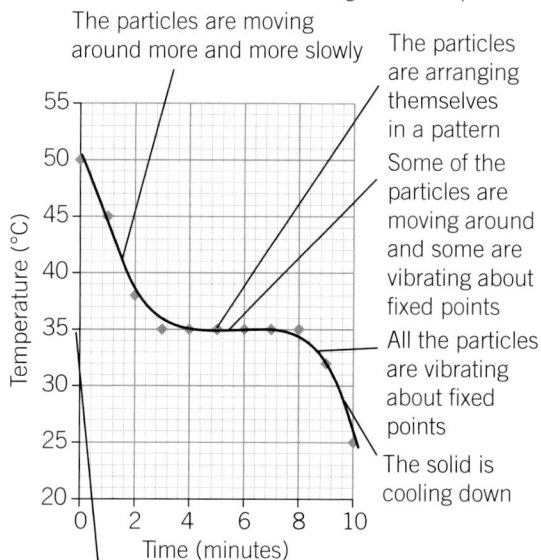

The particles are moving around more and more slowly

The particles are arranging themselves in a pattern

Some of the particles are moving around and some are vibrating about fixed points

All the particles are vibrating about fixed points

The solid is cooling down

This is the melting point of the substance

5.1.4

A gas, gas, liquid, conserved, boiling

B xenon, mercury, mercury

C bromine at 20 °C – liquid; mercury at 400 °C – gas; xenon at −115 °C – solid

D **a** A, B, C   **b** A and C   **c** B   **d** B

5.1.5

A gas, surface, condensation, sublimation

B **a** independent – place (where the Petri dish is); dependent – time for all the water to evaporate; control – amount of water

 b to ensure that the investigation is a fair test

C **a** 1, 5, 2   **b** 2, 6, 3

 c 3, 8, 4, 2   **d** 3, 7, 9, 2

5.1.6

A mixing, gas, diffusion, stir

B **a** particles spread out throughout the room and randomly arranged

 b the particles move randomly in the air all the time

C **a** dependent; control; independent; control

 b it is difficult to judge exactly when the purple colour has completely spread out

 c the size of crystals can vary considerably, and it is difficult to pick out crystals that are all the same size

 d as temperature increases, the time for the purple colour to spread out will be less

 e the higher the temperature, the faster the particles move

5.1.7

A all, collide, force, pressure

B there are fewer particles in jar **Y**, so collisions with the walls of the container are less frequent

C from top – true; not possible to know; true; not possible to know; false; true

D e.g. the particles move more slowly, so they hit the walls less frequently and less strongly

5.1.8

A one, compounds, cannot, one, two, strongly, atom, molecule

B 1, 4

C **a** A, D, F   **b** A   **c** D and F

 d B, C, E   **e** D and F   **f** B and E

D **a** two white circles, touching each other

 b one red circle in the middle, with two white circles touching it

 c one black atom, with four white circles touching it

 d one blue circle and one red circle, touching each other

 e one blue circle in the middle, with two red circles touching it

5.2.1

A pure, sharp, impure, temperatures, more, not, mixture, properties / melting points

B pure substances – X and Z; reason – their melting points are sharp / they do not melt over a range of temperatures

C a i S **ii** P **iii** R **iv** Q

   b diagram showing two types of particle, each made up of two or more types of atom (circles of different colours / with different shading)

D sand and water – filtration – sand does not dissolve in water; sand and steel nails – magnet – steel is attracted to magnets, but sand is not; flour and marbles – sieve – each piece of flour is small enough to go through holes in sieve, but marbles are not

5.2.2

A solution, solute, solvent, solute, move, cannot, same, liquid, gas

B examples of suitable sentences:

   a Sugar dissolves in solvents such as water.

   b When you mix sugar and water and stir, sugar is the solute and water is the solvent.

   c Sugar dissolves in water to make a solution.

C a box showing bigger sugar particles surrounded by smaller water particles; water particles are touching but randomly arranged

   b sugar particles separate from each other and spread out; the sugar particles are surrounded by water particles

D a 1000 g + 12 g = 1012 g **b** 156 g – 7 g = 149 g

   c 1004.6 g – 9.0 g = 995.6 g

E a nail polish is soluble in propanone, but not in water

   b solvent – water; solutes – carbon dioxide, sugar, flavourings

5.2.3

A saturated, solubility, soluble, soluble

B a 3, 4, 2, 5, 1

   b final mass of solution (measured in step 5) minus 100 g

   c variable – volume / mass / amount of water; reason – so that the test is fair

C a straight line, drawn with a ruler, that passes through, or close to, all the points

   b 2, 3

5.2.4

A different, physical, filtering, insoluble, dissolved, liquid, filtrate, residue

B 3, 2, 5, 4, 1 **or** 3, 4, 1, 2, 5

C a 1 – ✓ – pieces of dirt – oil; **2** – ✓ – undissolved potassium chloride – potassium chloride solution; **3** – ✓ – ground-up coffee beans – coffee solution; **4** – ✗

   b 1 / 2 / 3 – pieces of dirt / undissolved potassium chloride / ground-up coffee beans too big to fit through holes in filter; oil particles / particles in solution small enough to fit through holes

D a it shows that the filtrate particles (flour) are small enough to go through the holes in the filter paper (sieve) but the residue particles (marbles) are too big to go through the holes

   b you cannot see individual particles in a real filtrate, but you can see individual pieces of flour

E solubility at 80 °C = 167 g/100 g of water and solubility at 20 °C = 33 g/100 g of water.

so maximum residue on cooling = 167 g – 33 g = 134 g

5.2.5

A evaporation, solid, solute, distillation, condensation, solution

B clockwise from top-left: 5, 1, 2, 4, 3

C a 1 – both; **2** – evaporation; **3** – both; **4** – distillation; **5** – both

   b e.g. in both processes, the solvent changes state from liquid to gas; in evaporation, the solvent vapour is not usually collected but in distillation the solvent evaporates, condenses, and is collected

D a water

   b in evaporation, the solvent – in this case water – evaporates and escapes; in order to collect the solvent, the vapour would need to be collected and cooled so that it condenses and can be collected as a liquid

5.2.6

A solvent, chromatography, different, spot

B a 2 **b** they are both soluble in the solvent

   c one is more strongly attracted to the paper, or dissolves better in the solvent, than the other

   d chlorophyll and carotene

   e there could be other pigments that travel the same distance up the paper in these conditions

C there are no reactants in the reaction mixture, so the reactants must have finished reacting

Big Idea 5 Pinchpoint

A this is an incorrect answer – the particles **do** touch their neighbours in the liquid state

B this is an incorrect answer – oxygen is in the **liquid** state at −200 °C, not in the gas state; the particles are **not** far apart from each other – they are touching their neighbours; the particles do **not** move throughout the container, they move randomly at the bottom of the container

C this is the correct answer

D this is an incorrect answer – oxygen is in the **liquid** state at −200 °C, so its particles are **not** arranged in a pattern – they are arranged randomly; the particles are **not** far apart from each other – they are touching their neighbours; the particles do **not** vibrate on the spot – they move around randomly all over the place, sliding over each other

Pinchpoint follow-up

A **a** **i** the particles are randomly arranged; the particles are at the bottom of the container

ii the particles are not touching each other

b diagram showing particles randomly arranged at the bottom of the box; the particles should be touching their neighbours

B from top – gas, liquid, solid, gas, solid, solid

C 58 – random and touching – random, sliding over each other; –5 – random and touching – random, sliding over each other; 60 – random and far apart – random, throughout the container; –10 – regular pattern – vibrating on the spot

D **a** solid – particles arranged in a regular pattern, touching each other; liquid – particles arranged randomly in bottom of box, touching each other; gas – particles arranged randomly, throughout the box, not touching each other

b in the solid state, the particles vibrate on the spot; in the liquid state, the particles move around randomly, sliding over each other; in the gas state, the particles move around randomly, throughout the container

6.1.1

A new, rearranged, differently, not, energy, physical

B **a** **W** and **Z**

b in **W** and **Z**, the atoms are joined together differently before and after the reaction

C from top: chemical; physical; both; chemical

D chemical change; reasons: bright flame, showing that energy has been transferred to the surroundings; it is likely to be difficult to get shiny magnesium metal back from the white powder that is present at the end

E chemical reactions make new substances, but physical changes do not; physical changes are normally easy to reverse, but chemical reactions are difficult to reverse; both physical changes and chemical reactions involve energy changes; in chemical reactions, the atoms are joined together differently after the reaction; in physical changes the atoms are joined together in the same way before and after the reaction

6.1.2

A sour, soapy, corrosive, skin, irritants, dilute

B from top – wear eye protection; burning your skin

C **a** the acid in bottle **X** is more corrosive than in **Y**

b there are more acid particles in bottle **X** than **Y**

c add water to bottle **X**

D **a** the particles produced by both acids and alkalis contain hydrogen atoms

b the particles in alkalis include oxygen atoms but the particles in acids do not; the particles in alkalis have a negative charge but the particles in acids have a positive charge

6.1.3

A neutral, blue, red, neutral, alkaline, pH, less / lower, neutral, more / greater

B from top: alkaline, acidic, alkaline

C **a** it is difficult to judge which colour on the pH chart exactly matches the colour observed in the test solution

b pH probe attached to data logger

D **a** X, W, U, Z, V, Y **b** V, Y, Z

c **Y** – the most concentrated solution of acid is most acidic, so its pH is lowest

6.1.4

A all, some, strong, weak, litre

B hydrochloric – 1; ethanoic – 4; sulfuric – 2; citric – 4

C **a** In a solution of a strong acid, **all** the acid particles split up.

b In a solution of a weak acid, **only some of** the acid particles split up.

c A concentrated solution of ethanoic acid has **more** acid dissolved in it than a dilute solution of ethanoic acid.

d A concentrated solution of hydrochloric acid has a **lower** pH than a dilute solution of hydrochloric acid.

e The pH of a strong acid is **lower** than the pH of a weak acid, if the concentration of two acids is the same.

f The pH of an acid solution depends on acid strength **and the concentration of the solution**.

D **a** wear goggles and do not let the solution touch the skin

b Dan; there will still be hazards associated with using the solution, and it is better to take too many safety precautions than too few

6.1.5

A neutralised, increases, decreases

B **a** increases

b so that he can grow crops that thrive at the new pH

c neutralising acidic lakes **or** using a base to remove excess stomach acid

C independent – type of tablet; dependent – volume / amount of acid that the tablet neutralises; control – temperature, concentration of acid, type of acid, mass of tablet

D top right – **W**, **Z**; middle – **Y**; bottom right – **V**, **X**

6.1.6

A salt, chloride, sulfate, hydrogen

B 4, 6, 2, 1, 5, 7, 3

C clockwise, from left: copper sulfate solution, evaporating basin, beaker, boiling water

D **a** magnesium sulfate **b** zinc chloride

c copper chloride **d** sodium sulfate

e potassium chloride

E **a** **X**

b the solution of acid **X** reacts with zinc, but the solution of acid **Y** does not; this means that solution **X** must be the stronger and/or more concentrated acid, so it has the lower pH

6.2.1

A cannot, one, metals, metal, electricity, high

B **three** from: metals are good conductors of electricity, but non-metals are not; metals are good conductors of heat, but non-metals are not; metals are shiny, but non-metals are dull; metals have high densities, but non-metals have low densities; metals are malleable and ductile, but non-metals are brittle

C **a** **Q** and **R**

    b **S**; it is shiny, conducts electricity and has a high density, like most other metals; it is liquid at room temperature, unlike most other metals

    c **Q** and **R**   **d** **Q**

    e **T**; conducts electricity; solid at room temperature

    f **Q**; only one in the gas state at room temperature

6.2.2

A oxides, oxidation, non-metal, solid, gas, acidic, reactants, products, right, make / produce

B top – oxygen molecule; bottom, from left – reactant molecules, product molecules

C **a** magnesium + oxygen → magnesium oxide

    b nitrogen + oxygen → nitrogen dioxide

    c potassium + oxygen → potassium peroxide

    d sulfur + oxygen → sulfur dioxide

D nitrogen dioxide and sulfur dioxide

6.2.3

A metals, electricity, hydrogen, magnesium

B **a** magnesium – many bubbles quickly formed; zinc – bubbles formed, but fewer than for magnesium; iron – bubbles formed, but slightly fewer than for zinc

    b e.g. all the metals react with dilute acid; the reaction with magnesium was most **vigorous**; the reaction with iron was least **vigorous**; this shows that magnesium is the most **reactive** of the three metals; the gas in the bubbles is **hydrogen**

C **a** magnesium chloride   **b** zinc sulfate

    c iron chloride

D **a** magnesium + hydrochloric acid →
                      magnesium chloride + hydrogen

    b zinc + sulfuric acid → zinc sulfate + hydrogen

    c iron + hydrochloric acid → iron chloride + hydrogen

E **a** magnesium – 15; zinc – 9; copper – 0

    b the more reactive the metal, the greater the temperature increase when the metal reacts with hydrochloric acid

6.2.4

A air, reactive, oxide, oxide, unreactive, reactions, vigorously

B e.g. in the experiment, the metal that burns most vigorously is magnesium – this means that magnesium is the most reactive metal in the experiment; the product of the reaction is magnesium oxide; one metal, copper, does not burn in air – instead, it forms a layer of copper oxide on its surface; copper is less reactive than magnesium, zinc, and iron; gold does not react with oxygen at all – it is the least reactive metal in the group

C **a** magnesium, zinc, iron, copper, gold

    b the metal with the most vigorous reaction is at the top, followed by the metal with the next most vigorous reaction, and so on; gold is at the bottom since it does not react with oxygen when heated in a Bunsen flame

D **Y**; it does not form a non-conducting layer of metal oxide on its surface when exposed to air

6.2.5

A metals, top, unreactive, hydrogen, hydroxides

B **a** magnesium – not vigorous, tiny bubbles formed very slowly – hydrogen – magnesium hydroxide; potassium – very vigorous indeed – hydrogen – potassium hydroxide

    b magnesium reacts very slowly indeed with water, but potassium reacts violently with water; in both cases, one product is hydrogen gas; the reaction of water with magnesium makes magnesium hydroxide solution and the reaction of water with potassium makes potassium hydroxide solution

C **a** put some water in three test tubes; add a different metal to each test tube, and observe what happens; control variables – **two** from: amount / mass / size of metal; amount / volume / mass of water; temperature of water

    b the metal that reacts most vigorously is the one closest to the top of the reactivity series, so must be calcium; the one that does not react must be the one closest to the bottom of the reactivity series, i.e. silver; the third metal is then magnesium

6.2.6

A more, less, iron oxide, oxide, iron

B **a** Magnesium is **above** copper in the reactivity series.

    b Magnesium is **more** reactive than copper.

    c Magnesium displaces copper from its compound, copper **sulfate**.

    d As the reaction takes place, the colour of the blue copper sulfate solution gets **paler**.

    e As the reaction takes place, the piece of magnesium gets **smaller**.

C **1** – ✗ – copper (the metal on its own) is less reactive than magnesium (the metal in the compound); **2** – ✓ – magnesium (the metal on its own) is more reactive than lead (the metal in the compound); **3** – ✓ – zinc (the metal on its own) is more reactive than lead (the metal in the compound)

D **a** from left: oxygen atom, magnesium atom, copper atom

    b magnesium displaces copper from its compound, copper oxide, to make magnesium oxide and copper

E **a** zinc is more reactive than copper, so it displaces copper from copper sulfate solution; copper appears as a pink-brown solid, and the solution becomes paler as copper sulfate in solution is replaced by zinc sulfate in solution

b iron, the metal on its own, is less reactive than aluminium, the metal in the compound, and so it cannot displace aluminium from its compounds

Big Idea 6 Pinchpoint

A this is an incorrect answer – the pH **increases** after adding sodium hydroxide solution

B this is an incorrect answer – adding water or alkali both make a solution less acidic, so **increasing** its pH

C this is the correct answer

D this is an incorrect answer – adding water makes a solution less acidic, so **increasing** its pH

Pinchpoint follow-up

A
- **a** Adding water to an acid makes the solution **more** dilute / less **concentrated**.
- **b** When an acid is diluted, it has **fewer** acid particles per litre. (or converse answer)
- **c** The greater the number of acid particles per litre, the **lower** the pH. (or converse answer)
- **d** Adding alkali to an acid **neutralises** some or all of the acid.
- **e** Neutralising an acid **increases** the pH of the solution.
- **f** Adding water to an alkaline solution makes the solution **more** dilute.
- **g** Neutralising an alkali **decreases** the pH of the solution.
- **h** The smaller the number of acid particles per litre, the **higher** the pH.
- **i** When an alkali is diluted, its pH **decreases**.

B
- **a** 1 **b** 14 **c** 5 **d** 9
- **e** 7 **f** 1 **g** 9

C
- **a** adding water to an alkaline solution – pH decreases, but not below 7 – the solution has been diluted so there are fewer particles of alkali per litre; adding acid to an alkaline solution – pH decreases, possibly below 7 – some of the alkali has been neutralised so there are fewer particles of alkali per litre; adding water to an acidic solution – pH increases, but not above 7 – the solution has been diluted so there are fewer particles of acid per litre; adding alkali to an acidic solution – pH increases, possibly above 7 – some of the acid has been neutralised so there are fewer particles of acid per litre
- **b i** pH of the mixture is less than that of **X**
   - **ii** the concentration of hydrochloric acid in the mixture is greater than the concentration of hydrochloric acid in solution **X**

D 1, 3, 5

7.1.1

A layers, inner, outer, mantle, solid, flow, crust, minerals

B e.g. the outer and inner core are both mainly iron and nickel, but the outer core is liquid and the inner core is solid; the crust, mantle, and inner core are all solid, but they are made of different materials; both the mantle and outer core can flow

C a two from: the layer on the outside of the Earth and egg is relatively thin; the layer on the outside of Earth and egg is solid; the Earth and egg are made up of separate layers; the layer that is in the very middle is solid

- **b two** from: the egg is egg-shaped but the shape of the Earth is closer to spherical; the Earth has a liquid outer core, which is not shown in the egg model

D a mass of silicon $= \dfrac{28}{100} \times 24$ trillion tonnes

$= 6.7$ trillion tonnes (to 2 sig. fig.)

- **b** percentage of the element $= \dfrac{1.3}{24} \times 100 = 5.4\%$;

the nearest to this is 5.6%, which is iron

7.1.2

A metamorphic, soft, biological, sediments, transport, deposition, strata, compaction, cementation (either order), compaction, squashes, cementation

B a biological – the breaking up or wearing down of rock by the action of living things; chemical – the breaking up or wearing down of a rock by the action of substances, e.g. those in rainwater; physical – the breaking up or wearing down of rock, e.g. because of changing temperature

- **b** the movement of sediments far from their original rock

C porous – there are gaps between the grain because sedimentary rocks were formed from separate sediments; soft – the forces holding the grains together are not very strong because the sediments were joined together by compaction or cementation

D a compaction
- **b** in both the model and the formation of some types of sedimentary rock, the weight of something above the sediments squashes together the sediments below
- **c** e.g. the 1 kg weight in the model is different from reality, in which layers of sediments above squash together the sediments below

7.1.3

A magma, lava, solidifies / freezes, crystals, non-porous, hard, pressure, crystals

B a warm – bigger crystals formed – particles have more time to arrange themselves into crystals; cold – smaller crystals formed – particles have less time to arrange themselves into crystals

- **b** underground, liquid rock cools more slowly than liquid rock on the surface, so the crystals are bigger in igneous rock formed underground

C not porous – no gaps between crystals – formed from liquid that cools and solidifies; hard – strong forces between particles – formed from liquid that cools and solidifies

D a sedimentary, because fossils are sometimes present in sedimentary rock, but never in igneous rock
- **b** the action of high pressure, because the action of heat would destroy the fossil **or** because the action of high pressure distorts the shape of the fossil

7.1.4

A recycled, sedimentary, freezes / solidifies, igneous, temperatures / heating, metamorphic, uplift

B

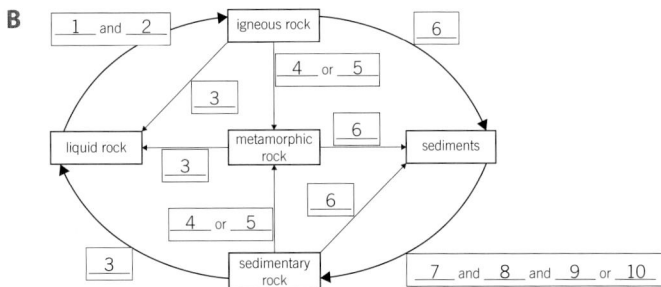

C e.g. plant roots grow in a crack in the rock, eventually forcing small pieces of rock to break off; the sediments are transported in a stream to the sea; the sediments are deposited, and form sedimentary rock by compaction; the sedimentary rock is close to some magma, and warms up; particles in the sediments move, and form crystals of metamorphic rock

7.1.5

A metal, metal, high, insulators, physical, alkalis

B **a** 3 **b** 1 **c** 2

C **a** Y

   b Y has typical ceramic properties (including high melting point, brittle, electrical insulator)

D **a** the ceramic material

   b the position of the masses and the size of the piece of ceramic material

   c to hold the ceramic material firmly in position

   d this 'measuring instrument' has a greater resolution

   e ensure that the masses will fall on the table when the ceramic block breaks, not onto people's feet

7.2.1

A orbit, natural, planets, Sun, Solar System, stars, galaxy, Milky Way, Universe, stars, exoplanets, light year

B **a** distances in space are huge; one light year is over 9 million million kilometres, so the light year is more convenient for these distances

   b other planets within our Solar System – years; next neighbouring star beyond the Sun – cannot be reached; Andromeda, our neighbouring galaxy – cannot be reached; the Moon – days

C Proxima Centauri - nearest star (other than the Sun) – 4 light-years; Moon – 1 light-second; Andromeda – nearest large galaxy (other than the Milky Way) – 2 million light-years; Sun – 8 light-minutes

D **asteroids** are some of the smallest objects in our **Solar System**; they orbit the **Sun**; **Moons** orbit **planets**; many **moons** are larger than most **asteroids**; **planets** are larger than **moons**; they orbit the **Sun**; the **Sun** and everything that orbits it make up the **Solar System**; billions of stars group together to make up our galaxy, the **Milky Way**; billions of galaxies together make up the **Universe**

7.2.2

A 8, solar system, Sun, elliptical, reflection, Venus, rocky, Uranus, gaseous, hotter, colder, asteroid, dwarf

B **a** emits own light – Sun; reflects light from another object – planets, moons

   b emit, reflect, Sun, orbit, Sun

C **a** all planets nearer the Sun (out to Mars) are rocky and small, lack rings, have few or no moons, and are hotter; all planets further from the Sun (from Jupiter onwards) are large gas giants, have rings, have many moons, and are colder

   b Neptune is far from the Sun so expect it to be a gas giant, large (50 000 km diameter; if value given, accept 20 000–150 000), cold (−210 °C; accept −270 to −200), with rings, and many moons (14; accept 10–80)

7.2.3

A day / 24 hours, spins, night, year, orbits, tilt, towards, more, constellations, different, Sun, year

B the Moon – orbits the Earth once a month; the Sun – the Earth spins on its axis once every 24 hours and so different regions of the Earth face the Sun at different times of day; stars – the Earth orbits the Sun once a year and the night-side of the Earth faces different constellations of stars during the year

C **a** Accra will be hottest and Iqaluit coldest, with the others in order of how far north they are; reason: the Sun is nearest to being overhead at Accra so each bit of ground receives more of the Sun's rays; (or converse: Sun lowest over horizon at Iqaluit, etc.)

   b Accra: 12.4 hours (accept 12.0–14.3); Iqaluit: 20.8 hours (accept 18.0–24.0)

D there would no difference in day-length and little, if any, difference in temperature between summer and winter; it would still be cooler than at the equator and hotter than the poles

7.2.4

A Sun, Earth, phases, Earth, geocentric, heliocentric

B 1 – C; 2 – G; 3 – F; 4 – A; 5 – B; 6 – D; 7 – H; 8 – E

C first quarter; full; third quarter; waning crescent; new

D **a** 2 **b** 3, 4 (row 1 is blank)

E **a** full moon **b** new moon

Big Idea 7 Pinchpoint

A this is an incorrect answer – **planets** orbit the **Sun**

B this is the correct answer

C this is an incorrect answer – solar systems are **smaller** than galaxies

D this is an incorrect answer – solar systems are **inside** galaxies

Pinchpoint follow-up

A **three** from: planet, asteroid, comet, meteor

B option 3 is correct (in option 1 the order of all values has been reversed; in option 2 all values are too small)

C

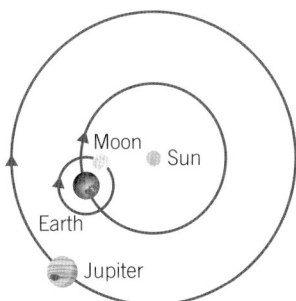

D Proxima Centauri – 4 ✓; Sun – 2 ✓; Jupiter – 3 ✓; Moon – 1 ✓; Andromeda galaxy – 5 ✗

Section 2 Revision questions

1 **a** a substance that cannot be broken down into other substances **or** a substance that is made of one type of atom [1]

   b Au [1]

   c in the solid state, particles are arranged in a regular pattern and vibrating on the spot [1]; when a substance sublimes, particles leave their positions in the regular pattern and escape to the surroundings as separate particles, moving around from place to place throughout the container [1]

   d in a physical change, no new substance is made but in a chemical reaction, new substances are made [1]; since no new substance is made, subliming is a physical change [1]

2 **a** sugar [1] **b** 102 g – 95 g [1] = 7 g [1]

3 **a** Thursday [1]

   b an acid [1] to neutralise / remove excess alkali / base [1]

   c wear eye protection [1]

4 **a** sulfuric acid [1]

   b zinc oxide + sulfuric acid → zinc sulfate + water [1]

   c zinc oxide [1]

   d heat over a water bath **or** stop heating when about half the water has evaporated and leave in a warm place for a few days [1]

   e wear eye protection [1], do not touch hot apparatus [1]

5 **a** base [1] **b** 11 in bottom row [1]

   c $\dfrac{10 + 9 + 10}{3}$ [1] = 9.67 [1]

   d the independent variable is categoric [1]

   e tablet **X** neutralises the greatest volume of acid [1]

6 **a** add small pieces of each metal to big trough of water [1] and observe vigour of reaction – the metal that reacts most vigorously is most reactive [1]; control variables – size of metal [1], volume / amount of water [1]

   b **one** from: place a protective screen between reaction vessel and class [1]; do not touch the metals [1]

7 copper and silver nitrate solution [1]; magnesium and copper chloride solution [1]

8 **a** a material that water can soak into [1]

   b there are small gaps between the sediments that the rock is made from [1]

9 **a** the sedimentary rock melts [1] and freezes [1]

   b the igneous rock is weathered [1] and the resulting sediments transported [1]; sedimentation then occurs [1] followed by compaction or cementation (to make the sediments join together) [1]

10 the Earth is spinning on its axis (or rotating, throughout) [1]; the Moon and stars moved (almost) the same amount in Figure 3 (or in one hour) due to rotation of Earth [1]; stars are back to (almost) same position in Figure 4 (or in one day) because the Earth takes one day to spin [1]; the Moon has shifted position compared to the stars in Figure 4 (or in one day) because the Moon is orbiting the Earth [1]

11 both evaporation and boiling are changes of state from liquid to gas [1]; boiling involves the formation of bubbles, but evaporation does not [1]; in evaporation, particles leave the liquid surface [1] but in boiling, bubbles of gas also form throughout the liquid, rise to the surface and escape [1]; boiling occurs at the boiling point only [1] but evaporating happens at any temperature [1]

12 from top: a pure element, a mixture of two elements, a mixture of an element and a compound, a mixture of two elements [3 for all correct; 2 for 2 correct; 1 for 1 correct]

13 **a** liquid, solid, solid [1]

   b all three elements are shiny and silver-coloured [1]; mercury is liquid at 20 °C but platinum and silver are in the solid state at 20 °C [1]; mercury and platinum do not react with substances in the air, but silver does [1]

   c they are both solid, shiny, and silver-coloured [1]

   d platinum does not react with substances in the air, but silver reacts with hydrogen sulfide in polluted air to make an unattractive black substance [1]

   e mercury is in the liquid state at 20 °C but platinum is in the solid state (the action of tilting moves a liquid and triggers the alarm, but would not affect a solid) [1]

14 300 000 000 × 60 × 60 × 24 × 365 [1]
= 9 460 000 000 000 000 (or 9.46×10^{15}) [1] m (to 3 sig. fig.)

15 **a** quarter: 7 [1] **b** full: 15 or 16 [1]

16 exoplanet A: mass – accept range 0.1–10 [1]; type – rocky [1]; exoplanet B: mass – accept range 30–3000 [1]; type – gas giant [1]

8.1.1

A multi-cellular, hierarchy, tissues, organ, organ system, organism

B **a** group of similar cells working together

   b group of different tissues working together

   c group of different organs working together

C red blood cell – cell; blood – tissue; heart – organ; circulatory system – organ system; dog – organism

D muscle tissue – contracts to pump blood around the body **or** nervous tissue – stimulates heart to beat

E to transport substances (such as glucose and oxygen) to internal cells; to allow cells to communicate with each other; to co-ordinate the activities of the organism

8.1.2

A skeleton, protect, support, move, blood, marrow, muscular skeletal

B 1 skull; 2 jaw bone; 3 collar bone; 4 vertebral column; 5 radius; 6 femur; 7 kneecap

C muscles are attached to bones; when a muscle contracts it pulls on the bone, causing it to move; joints are where two or more bones join together, and allow bones to move in different directions / independently of other parts of the skeleton

D support – bones create a framework for muscles and organs to connect; protection – stop vital organs from being damaged; making blood – tissue in centre of some bones makes blood cells

E **one** from: skull – brain; vertebral column – spinal cord; ribcage – heart / lung

8.1.3

A joints, movement, directions, ligaments, cartilage, contracts, force, newtons

B **a** shoulder is a ball-and-socket joint, which allows movement in all directions; knee joint is a hinge, which allows movement backwards and forwards

    b the joints are fixed so no movement can occur

C push down as hard as possible onto a newton scale; the reading on the newton scale will be the force exerted by the triceps muscle

D **a** clockwise from bottom-left: ligaments, fluid, cartilage, tendon

    b tendon – connects muscle to bone; ligament – connects two bones together; cartilage – smooth tissue that protects the ends of the bone; fluid – makes joint slippery, allowing bones to move without rubbing

    c bone marrow

8.1.4

A tendons, shortens, bone, muscles, joint, antagonistic, relaxes

B **a** to pump blood around the body

    b to squeeze food along the digestive system

    c to cause movement

C pairs of muscles that work together to cause movement at a joint; when one muscle contracts, the other relaxes

D **a** muscle B contracts and muscle A relaxes

    b muscle C contracts and muscle D relaxes

E when a muscle can no longer contract with the same force (occurs after repeated muscle use)

8.2.1

A cells, microscope, magnifies, observation

B slide – **Y**; eyepiece lens – **W**; objective lens – **X**; light – **Z**

C **a** select the objective lens with the lowest magnification; look through the eyepiece and turn the coarse-focus knob slowly until the leaf comes into view; turn the fine-focus knob until the leaf is focused

    b use an objective lens with a higher magnification

    c total magnification = eye piece lens magnification × objective lens
= 10 × 50 = ×500 magnification

8.2.2

A nucleus, cytoplasm, cell membrane, mitochondria, cell wall, chloroplasts, vacuole

B animal – clockwise from top-left: cell membrane, cytoplasm, mitochondrion, nucleus; plant – clockwise from top-left: chloroplast, vacuole, cytoplasm, mitochondrion, cell wall, cell membrane, nucleus

C nucleus – contains genetic material and controls the cell; mitochondria – where respiration occurs; cell membrane – barrier that controls what comes into and out of a cell; cytoplasm – where chemical reactions take place

D **a** where photosynthesis occurs

    b contains cell sap to keep the cell firm

    c strengthens the cell and provide support

E cellulose

8.2.3

A specialised, red blood, impulses, sperm, hair, water, chloroplasts

B **a** egg cell   **b** nerve cell   **c** leaf / palisade cell

C **a** true   **b** false – they have **no** nucleus (to maximise their ability to carry oxygen)

    c true   **d** false – they contain **haemoglobin or** they **do not** contain chlorophyll

D **a** to allow the sperm to 'swim' towards the egg

    b to transfer energy for movement

    c to enable the cell to move through fluid more easily / to enter the egg more easily

E root hair cell – large surface area for absorbing water and nutrients

8.2.4

A high, low, diffusion, oxygen, carbon dioxide

B oxygen, glucose

C **B** should show partial mixing of the two types of particles; **C** should show both types of particles evenly distributed

D water diffuses into plant through root hair cells; it moves from the soil where it is in a high concentration to the cell where it is in a low concentration

E water will diffuse into the plant cells and fill up the vacuole; this pushes outwards on the cell wall and makes the cell rigid; this helps the plant to stand upright

8.2.5

A euglenas, uni-cellular, one, cytoplasm, chloroplasts, eye spot, flagellum

B step 1 – nucleus divides; step 2 – cytoplasm divides (a cell membrane is formed)

C **a** enables it to move / swim (towards light / food)

    b make food by photosynthesis

    c detects light (then euglena moves towards it)

D euglenas are only made of one cell; plants are multi-cellular organisms

E engulf / surround tiny particles of food (algae / bacteria / plant cells) forming a food vacuole; the food vacuole then digests the food

Big Idea 8 Pinchpoint

A this is the correct answer

B this is an incorrect answer – plants **do not** suck up water, it moves into the plant by diffusion

C this is an incorrect answer – particles move from an area of **high** concentration to an area of **low** concentration

D this is an incorrect answer – water (and other) molecules can move into **and** out of cells by diffusion

Pinchpoint follow-up

A **a** the larger the surface area, the greater the rate of diffusion
 b 5 (au)
 c the larger the surface area, the quicker the diffusion of useful substances (such as oxygen / glucose) into the cell, or waste products (such as CO_2) out of the cell

B water molecules **diffuse** from one region to another **because** they move from an area of high **concentration** to one of lower **concentration**; this means water moves from the soil to the cell, and then between the cells

C **a** kitchen box circled in first two lines; no box circled in third row **b** high, low, same

D **a** arrow coming from vacuole pointing to outside of the cell
 b water moves out of the cell as water is at a higher concentration inside the cell so diffuses to a lower concentration in salt water

9.1.1

A food chain, energy, producer, photosynthesis, consumers, prey, predator, food web, linked / interconnected, decomposers, soil

B food chain shows the transfer or energy between organisms; food web shows linked food chains

C **a** food chain beginning with the dandelion then 3 correct links, e.g. dandelion → grasshopper → spider → owl
 b producer: dandelion; herbivore: beetle / grasshopper / slug; carnivore: shrew / spider / mouse / owl; predator: shrew / spider / mouse / owl; prey: shrew / spider / mouse

D as energy is transferred along the food chain, much is transferred to the surroundings by heating and waste products; therefore, less energy is available at each level in a food chain

9.1.2

A interdependence, population, increase, bioaccumulation

B very small amounts of mercury enter plankton; fish eat many plankton; mercury accumulates (bioaccumulation) but level still safe for humans; shark eat many fish; mercury accumulates to a level that is toxic

C initially lionfish ate many native fish so lionfish population increased and native fish population decreased; eventually not enough food for lionfish so their population decreased; fewer native fish now eaten so their population increases, more food now available for lionfish so cycle starts again

D wolf population eats the elk population, decreasing their numbers; this means less willow is eaten by elks so more is available for the beavers; the beavers use willow to make dams, which affect the water flow in rivers and streams

9.1.3

A habitat, community, ecosystem, co-exist, niche

B **a** food sources / niches; parts of the tree
 b habitat: oak tree; community: birds, ants, squirrels, woodlice, slugs, and oak tree

C **a** **i** quadrat   **ii** hedgerow
 b more light / water / space further from the hedgerow
 c you have not chosen where to place the quadrat, e.g. an interesting area – sample locations were selected before starting

9.1.4

A resources, mates, food, light, minerals, interdependence, increases, food

B **three** from: light – for photosynthesis; water – for photosynthesis and to keep their cells rigid; space – so roots can absorb enough water and leaves can absorb enough light; minerals––to make chemicals needed for healthy growth

C **a** space **or** mates
 b space – to hunt / for shelter; mates – to reproduce
 c original population would decrease as it has less food, or moves to a new area to find food /
original population not affected if it was the stronger competitor

D **a** solid line – rabbits; dashed line – foxes
 b Y, Z
 c **Y** – an increasing fox population means that more rabbits are eaten so rabbit population decreases
Z – as number of rabbits increases, the number of foxes will also increase as they have more food available

9.2.1

A pollen, anther, insects, brightly, nectar, sweet, large, light / low mass, stigma

B 1 filament; 2 anther; 3 petal; 4 stigma; 5 style; 6 ovary; 7 sepal

C transfer of pollen from the anther to the stigma (by wind or insects)

D **three** from: brightly coloured petals – to attract insects; nectar – sweet sugary fluid which bees can use to make honey; produce sticky / spiky pollen – stick to insects;

anther / stigma found within flower – so insects can brush against them

E wind – pollen has low mass so can be blown easily by wind; lots produced to increase chance of it reaching another plant; insect – larger mass, less produced; sticky / spiky exterior to stick to insects

9.2.2

A fertilisation, pollen, ovule, fruit, seeds, germinate, warmth

B 1 ovule; 2 ovule nucleus; 3 pollen grain; 4 pollen nucleus

C the pollen grain grows a pollen tube down the style until it reaches an ovule inside the ovary; the nucleus of the pollen grain then travels down the tube and joins with the ovule nucleus (fertilisation); the ovary then develops into the fruit and the ovules become seeds

D 1. seed swells and hard **seed coat** splits; 2. first **root** appears (and grows downwards); 3. first **shoot** appears (and grows upwards towards the **light**); 4. plant starts to make its own food by photosynthesis

E $\frac{18}{25} \times 100 = 72\%$

9.2.3

A dispersed, competition, space, wind, animals

B a wind – seed is light, and extensions act as parachutes / wings (keeping seed in air for longer so disperses further)

b explosive – fruits burst open when they are ripe, throwing seeds in different directions

C so they are spread far away from the parent plant and other seeds to minimise competition for space / nutrients / water / sunlight

D a the larger the wing of the seed, the further it will travel

b i length of seed wing, in cm

ii distance the seed travels, in cm or m

iii height seed is dropped from, in cm or m; height of fan, in cm or m; windspeed, in m/s; fan setting

Big Idea 9 Pinchpoint

A this is the correct answer

B this is an incorrect answer – this is the definition of **seed dispersal**

C this is an incorrect answer – this is the definition of **pollination**

D this is an incorrect answer – this answer is vague and lacks detail. The definition should refer to the **nuclei** of cells fusing together.

Pinchpoint follow-up

A wind-pollinated plant: anthers hang out of flower so pollen is blown in the wind; stigmas also hang out of the flower to catch pollen; covered in 'feathers' to help catch pollen; pollen grain grows tube down style to ovary; pollen nucleus travels down tube to ovary where it fuses with an ovule nucleus – fertilisation; fertilised ovule develops into seed

B seeds, pollen, wind, style, ovule, nucleus, fertilisation, fruit, dispersal

C 5, 4, 6, 1, 3, 2

D 1 – pollen tube grows from the pollen grain through the style; 2 – pollen nucleus travels down pollen tube; 3 – pollen nucleus fuses with ovule nucleus – fertilisation

10.1.1

A species, variation, inherited, environmental

B inherited – eye colour, blood group; environment – accent, pierced ears; combination of both – height, skin colour

C environmental variation is caused by an organism's surroundings, whereas inherited variation is caused by the genetic material a person inherits from their parents

D a they each inherit a different mixture of genetic material from their parents (inherited variation) so they share some characteristics with each other but not all

b environment now also has an influence on the kittens' appearance, e.g. amount of food eaten (environmental variation) affects the cats' mass

10.1.2

A discontinuous, bar chart, continuous, histogram

B continuous – leg length, fish mass, leaf surface area; discontinuous – blood group, flower colour, number of spots

C a a characteristic that can take any value within a range

b a characteristic that can only result in certain values

D a i continuous variation

ii caused by a mixture of inherited variation and environmental variation; the seedling may inherit the ability to be tall but this will only occur if you have nutrient-rich soil / enough light

b histogram

10.1.3

A adaptations, environment, leaves, fur / coats, adapted

B waxy layer – prevents water evaporating; fleshy stems – store water; widespread roots – collect water from a large area; spines – small surface area to reduce water loss

C plant – e.g. loses leaves in winter to save energy and fallen leaves provide warmth and protection to base of tree; animal – e.g. migration to warmer climate / somewhere with more food / hibernation / grow thicker fur

D only best adapted organisms will survive, e.g. faster animals, increasing the number of organisms in the species with that characteristic; eventually all members of the species will have the characteristic / organisms that are not well adapted will move or die

10.2.1

A adolescence, physical, puberty, sex hormones, taller, pubic / underarm, break / deepen, shoulders, periods, hips

B adolescence is the period of time when a child develops into an adult – it involves both physical and emotional changes; puberty refers only to the physical changes

C **boys** – voice deepens, hair grows on face and chest, shoulders widen, testes start to produce sperm; **girls** – breasts develop, periods start, hips widen, ovaries start to release egg cells; **both** – pubic / underarm hair grows, growth spurt, body odour

D a to make space for a baby to grow in the uterus

   b to be able to produce milk for a baby if she becomes pregnant

10.2.2

A sperm, vagina, testicles, sperm ducts, penis, egg, oviducts, uterus

B 1 cervix; 2 ovary; 3 oviduct; 4 uterus; 5 vagina

C 1 testicle; 2 sperm duct; 3 glands; 4 urethra; 5 penis; 6 scrotum

D a releases an egg cell each month / produces female sex hormones

   b ring of muscle which keeps baby in place until it is ready to be born

   c receives sperm during sexual intercourse / passage through which baby is born

E sperm cells are made in the **testicles** and released into the **sperm duct**; here they mix with fluid from the **glands** that provides nutrients to keep them alive; the mixture of sperm and fluid is called **semen**; semen is released through the **urethra** in the **penis** during ejaculation / sexual intercourse

10.2.3

A ovary, cilia, ejaculation, nucleus / nuclei, fertilisation, embryo, uterus, implantation

B (sperm released from penis) → vagina → cervix → uterus → oviduct

C divides several times to form a ball of cells / embryo; the embryo attaches to lining of uterus – implantation; here it continues to grow and develop into a baby

D a low sperm count / sperm that cannot swim properly, so less likelihood of a sperm cell meeting an egg

   b eggs not being released from ovaries / blocked oviduct, so less likelihood of an egg cell meeting a sperm cell

10.2.4

A uterus, gestation, 9, amniotic, oxygen, blood, placenta, umbilical cord, cervix, uterus, vagina

B a fetus develops from a fertilised egg, ready to be born

C 1 placenta; 2 umbilical cord; 3 uterus; 4 fetus; 5 amniotic fluid; 6 cervix

D a organ where substances pass between the mother's blood and the fetus's blood such as oxygen and carbon dioxide. It also acts as a barrier to prevent infections and harmful substances reaching the fetus

   b amniotic fluid acts as a shock absorber, protecting the fetus from any bumps

E mother's cervix relaxes, which causes it to open; uterus walls contract, pushing the baby through the cervix, through the vagina, and out of the body

10.2.5

A menstrual, egg, ovulation, lining, menstruation / a period

B day 1 – period / menstruation / blood from the uterus lining starts to be lost; day 5 – period / menstruation / bleeding

stops and uterus lining begins to regrow; day 14 – ovulation / egg is released from an ovary

C a lining of the uterus breaks down and the cycle starts again

   b fertilised egg attaches to uterus lining and the woman becomes pregnant, so no menstruation / period occurs; the uterus lining remains thick

D condom – barrier method – prevents sperm being released into vagina; contraceptive pill – contain hormones that stop ovulation / affect uterus lining; (or other appropriate examples with explanations)

Big Idea 10 Pinchpoint

A this is an incorrect answer – water absorption occurs quicker when there is a **larger** surface area

B this is the correct answer

C this is an incorrect answer – shape B has a **larger** surface area

D this is an incorrect answer – water absorption will happen more quickly in shape B as it has the larger surface area

Pinchpoint follow-up

A a

Faces	Shape A	Shape B
Top and bottom	$2 \times 4 = 8$	$2 \times 8 = 16$
Front and back	$2 \times 4 = 8$	$2 \times 4 = 8$
Left and right	$2 \times 4 = 8$	$2 \times 2 = 4$
Total	24	28

   b arctic fox has short ears with small surface area, to reduce heat loss; desert fox has large, thin ears which have much bigger surface area than arctic fox's ears; this large surface area maximises heat loss to keep the fox cool

B villi **increase** the surface area; this **increases** the rate at which nutrients can diffuse from intestine into blood

C a $(2 \times (2 \times 8)) = 32$; $(2 \times (2 \times 4)) = 16$;
     $(2 \times (4 \times 8)) = 64$
     $= 32 + 16 + 64 = 112 \text{ mm}^2$

   b bigger than

D evaporate, smaller than, B

Section 3 Revision questions

1 a **X** petal [1]; **Y** stigma [1]; **Z** filament [1]

   b i reproductive / sex cell [1]
     ii anther [1]   iii ovary [1]

   c insect-pollinated, e.g. tulip / daisy / sunflower [1]; wind-pollinated, e.g. grass / corn / wheat [1]

   d the nuclei of the pollen and ovule / male and female plant gametes [1] join together / fuse [1]

2 a nucleus – controls the activities of the cell [1]; vacuole – stores sap and helps to keep the cell firm [1]; cytoplasm – where the cell's chemical reactions take place [1]

   b [contain chlorophyll] to enable the plant to photosynthesise [1]

3 **a** **six** from: take thin slice of onion material [1]; place on slide [1]; add cover slip [1]; add stain to help view some structures [1]; move microscope stage to its lowest position [1]; place the slide on the stage [1]; select (the objective lens with) the lowest magnification [1]; look through the eyepiece [1]; adjust the coarse focus knob until the cells come into view [1]; then adjust the fine focus knob until the cells are in focus [1]; increase the magnification (use an objective lens with a higher magnification) to view structures more clearly / in more detail [1]

b sketch shows: a number of cells in a regular pattern [1]; a minimum of three correctly labelled components [3]

c **i** cellulose [1]

ii (the cellulose is strong, so the) cell wall is rigid [1] to provide support for the cell / plant [1]

4 **a** mean $= \dfrac{450 + 410 + 370}{3}$ [1]

$= 410$ [1] N [1]

b e.g. muscle fatigue [1]

c **three** from: the two muscles are antagonistic pairs [1]; as the biceps contracts, the triceps relaxes [1], moving the lower arm upwards [1]; as the triceps muscle contracts, the biceps muscle relaxes [1], moving the lower arm upwards [1]

5 **a** A [1] and C [1]

b $\dfrac{8}{20} \times 100$ [1] $= 40\%$ [1]

c **two** from: an animal will be attracted to eat the plant [1]; the sticky coating on the seeds will stick to the animal's body / fur [1]; the seeds will then be deposited in another area [1]

6 **a** days $14 \rightarrow 16$ [1]

b egg is released / ovulation occurs around day 14 [1]; egg only lives / remains in body for a few days [1]

c **six** from: sperm are released from testes (into sperm duct) [1]; semen / sperm releases from penis **into** vagina [1]; sperm swim through cervix / uterus [1]; egg released from ovary [1]; sperm meet egg in the oviduct [1]; sperm burrows into egg [1]; sperm and egg nuclei fuse to form fertilised egg [1]; egg divides a number of times to form an embryo (which implants in uterus wall) [1]

7 **a** X – anther [1]; Y – stigma / style [1]

b wind pollinated [1]; **three** from: anthers / stamen hang out of the flower – pollen released into wind [1]; stigmas hang out of the flower – to catch pollen blown in wind [1]; lots of pollen released – increase chance of successful pollination [1]; low mass / light pollen – easily carried by wind [1]; stigma is hairy / feathery to catch more pollen [1]

8 **a** to keep *Daphnia* alive / so *Daphnia* could get oxygen / respire [1]

b **i** $10 \times 4 = \times40$ [1]

ii **two** from: unicellular organisms consist of only one cell [1]; organs such as eye can be seen / many different cells present within body [1]; structure size too large (at ×40 magnification) for unicellular organism [1]

c **i** use higher magnification / more powerful microscope lens [1]

ii muscle cell [1] contracts to pump blood [1] **or** nerve cell [1] to stimulate contraction **or** red blood cell [1] to carry oxygen [1]

Periodic table

1	2												3	4	5	6	7	0
																		4 **He** helium 2
7 **Li** lithium 3	9 **Be** beryllium 4												11 **B** boron 5	12 **C** carbon 6	14 **N** nitrogen 7	16 **O** oxygen 8	19 **F** fluorine 9	20 **Ne** neon 10
23 **Na** sodium 11	24 **Mg** magnesium 12												27 **Al** aluminium 13	28 **Si** silicon 14	31 **P** phosphorus 15	32 **S** sulfur 16	35.5 **Cl** chlorine 17	40 **Ar** argon 18
39 **K** potassium 19	40 **Ca** calcium 20	45 **Sc** scandium 21	48 **Ti** titanium 22	51 **V** vanadium 23	52 **Cr** chromium 24	55 **Mn** manganese 25	56 **Fe** iron 26	59 **Co** cobalt 27	59 **Ni** nickel 28	63.5 **Cu** copper 29	65 **Zn** zinc 30		70 **Ga** gallium 31	73 **Ge** germanium 32	75 **As** arsenic 33	79 **Se** selenium 34	80 **Br** bromine 35	84 **Kr** krypton 36
85 **Rb** rubidium 37	88 **Sr** strontium 38	89 **Y** yttrium 39	91 **Zr** zirconium 40	93 **Nb** niobium 41	96 **Mo** molybdenum 42	[98] **Tc** technetium 43	101 **Ru** ruthenium 44	103 **Rh** rhodium 45	106 **Pd** palladium 46	108 **Ag** silver 47	112 **Cd** cadmium 48		115 **In** indium 49	119 **Sn** tin 50	122 **Sb** antimony 51	128 **Te** tellurium 52	127 **I** iodine 53	131 **Xe** xenon 54
133 **Cs** caesium 55	137 **Ba** barium 56	139 **La*** lanthanum 57	178 **Hf** hafnium 72	181 **Ta** tantalum 73	184 **W** tungsten 74	186 **Re** rhenium 75	190 **Os** osmium 76	192 **Ir** iridium 77	195 **Pt** platinum 78	197 **Au** gold 79	201 **Hg** mercury 80		204 **Tl** thallium 81	207 **Pb** lead 82	209 **Bi** bismuth 83	[209] **Po** polonium 84	[210] **At** astatine 85	[222] **Rn** radon 86
[223] **Fr** francium 87	[226] **Ra** radium 88	[227] **Ac*** actinium 89	[261] **Rf** rutherfordium 104	[262] **Db** dubnium 105	[266] **Sg** seaborgium 106	[264] **Bh** bohrium 107	[277] **Hs** hassium 108	[268] **Mt** meitnerium 109	[271] **Ds** darmstadtium 110	[272] **Rg** roentgenium 111	[285] **Cn** copernicium 112		[286] **Nh** nihonium 113	[289] **Fl** flerovium 114	[289] **Mc** moscovium 115	[293] **Lv** livermorium 116	[294] **Ts** tennessine 117	[294] **Og** oganesson 118

key

1 **H** hydrogen 1

relative atomic mass
atomic symbol
name
atomic (proton) number

*The lanthanides (atomic numbers 58–71) and the actinides (atomic numbers 90–103) have been omitted.

OXFORD
UNIVERSITY PRESS

Great Clarendon Street, Oxford, OX2 6DP, United Kingdom

Oxford University Press is a department of the University of Oxford. It furthers the University's objective of excellence in research, scholarship, and education by publishing worldwide. Oxford is a registered trade mark of Oxford University Press in the UK and in certain other countries

British Library Cataloguing in Publication Data
Data available

978-1-38-203014-4

10 9 8 7 6 5 4

Paper used in the production of this book is a natural, recyclable product made from wood grown in sustainable forests. The manufacturing process conforms to the environmental regulations of the country of origin.

Printed in China

Acknowledgements

The publisher and the authors would like to thank the following for permission to use their photographs:

Cover image: SergeyIT/Shutterstock; **p39**: Kukhmar/Shutterstock; **p122(T)**: outdoorsman/Shutterstock; **p122(M)**: nattanan726/ Shutterstock; **p122(B)**: STEVE GSCHMEISSNER/SCIENCE PHOTO LIBRARY.

All artwork by Aptara Inc., Q2A Media Services Ltd., and Phoenix Photosetting